UNDERSTANDING CONSUMER BEHAVIOR

———— ■ ————

Marketing Lessons Learned From
Understanding the Consumer Experience

UNDERSTANDING CONSUMER BEHAVIOR

Marketing Lessons Learned From Understanding the Consumer Experience

GAIL TOM

California State University, Sacramento

HARCOURT COLLEGE PUBLISHERS

Fort Worth   Philadelphia   San Diego   New York   Orlando   Austin   San Antonio
Toronto   Montreal   London   Sydney   Tokyo

PUBLISHER	Mike Roche
ACQUISITIONS EDITOR	Bill Schoof
MARKETING STRATEGIST	Beverly Dunn
PROJECT MANAGER	Angela Williams Urquhart

ISBN: 0-03-032121-2

Library of Congress Catalog Card Number: 00-107149

Address for Domestic Orders
Harcourt College Publishers, 6277 Sea Harbor Drive, Orlando, FL 32887-6777
800-782-4479

Address for International Orders
International Customer Service
Harcourt College Publishers, 6277 Sea Harbor Drive, Orlando, FL 32887-6777
407-345-3800
(fax) 407-345-4060
(e-mail) hbintl@harcourtbrace.com

Address for Editorial Correspondence
Harcourt College Publishers, 301 Commerce Street, Suite 3700, Fort Worth, TX 76102

Web Site Address
http://www.harcourtcollege.com

Printed in the United States of America

0 1 2 3 4 5 6 7 8 9   202   9 8 7 6 5 4 3 2 1

Harcourt College Publishers

To Stephanie, Ryan and Cal

for their support, encouragement

and sense of humor

THE HARCOURT SERIES IN MARKETING

Ingram, LaForge, Avila, Schwepker, and Williams
Sales Management: Analysis and Decision Making
Fourth Edition

Krugman, Reid, Dunn, and Barban
Advertising: Its Role in Modern Marketing
Eighth Edition

Lindgren and Shimp
Marketing: An Interactive Learning System

Oberhaus, Ratliffe, and Stauble
Professional Selling: A Relationship Process
Second Edition

Parente
*Advertising Campaign Strategy: A Guide to
   Marketing Communication Plans*
Second Edition

Reedy
Electronic Marketing

Rosenbloom
Marketing Channels: A Management View
Sixth Edition

Sandburg
Discovering Your Marketing Career CD-ROM

Schaffer
Applying Marketing Principles Software

Schaffer
The Marketing Game

Schellinck and Maddox
Marketing Research: A Computer-Assisted Approach

Schnaars
MICROSIM

Schuster and Copeland
*Global Business: Planning for Sales and
   Negotiations*

Sheth, Mittal, and Newman
Customer Behavior: Consumer Behavior and Beyond

Shimp
*Advertising and Promotions: Supplemental Aspects
   of Integrated Marketing Communications*
Fifth Edition

Stauble
Marketing Strategy: A Global Perspective

Talarzyk
Cases and Exercises in Marketing

Terpstra and Sarathy
International Marketing
Eighth Edition

Tom
*Understanding Consumer Behavior: Marketing
   Lessons Learned From Understanding the
   Consumer Experience*

Watson
Electronic Commerce

Weitz and Wensley
*Readings in Strategic Marketing Analysis,
   Planning, and Implementation*

Zikmund
Exploring Marketing Research
Seventh Edition

Zikmund
Essentials of Marketing Research

Harcourt College Outline Series

Peterson
Principles of Marketing

PREFACE

The premise of this book is that an understanding of the consumer experience is the basis of successful marketing. Marketers must walk like their consumers, talk like their consumers, and shop like their consumers. Marketers must understand how their consumers see, feel, and think about marketing. This book will provide a glimpse into the consumer's experience of marketing—the starting point for all marketing efforts.

THIS BOOK HAS THREE OBJECTIVES. First, this book can serve as a supplement to marketing and consumer behavior textbooks. It provides interesting and entertaining examples, illustrations, and applications that highlight consumer behavior concepts. In this way, students will understand the concepts more thoroughly.

Second, this book is a readable collection that illustrates clearly the dynamic relationship between an understanding of the consumer experience and marketing. The reader can begin reading the book anywhere that strikes his or her fancy, and this book need not be read chapter by chapter. Rather, the reader's interest can guide his or her journey through the book. The essence of the book is distilled into concentrated "Gold Nuggets," which summarize the sections of the book. A listing of these Gold Nuggets is featured at the beginning of the book. A quick reading of these can serve the reader as pointers to explore sections that are of particular interest.

Third, this book is complemented with Web support. A collection of Internet sites has been selected to provide an interesting and interactive method of illustrating consumer behavior principles, concepts, and marketing. I have written some Web site exercises to help students grasp the concepts of consumer behavior while they polish their technology skills. Along with these exercises, the companion Web site also provides some other online features, including the "Reading Room," which provides both students and instructors with access to local, national, and even national business news; "Marketing Topics," which contains extensive support for all Harcourt College business texts (including exercises, data, and various company profiles); "Marketing Careers," a page that contains information on how to get a job in the field of marketing; and "Time Management," which has information on how to best manage your time as a

x

student, how to study effectively, and how to balance study and leisure time. All of this can be found at **www.harcourtcollege.com**.

A WORD OF THANKS ...   This book would not have come about had it not been for my students. I thank them for their enthusiasm, interest, and provocative perspectives. Thanks also to my book team at Harcourt College Publishers. I greatly appreciate Bill Schoof, who shared my vision for this project, and Bobbie Bochenko, who helped in shaping, refining, and fine-tuning this book. Thanks to the production team of Angela Urquhart, Lisa Kelley, and Linda Blundell, who helped manage the project, keep it on track, and get it to the marketplace. Thanks also to Mike McConnell and Bruce Siebert at Graphic World Publishing Services for their hard work and enthusiasm.

This book was fun to write. I hope you have fun reading it.

Gail Tom
September 2000

ABOUT THE AUTHOR

Gail Tom (Ph.D., M.S., B.A., University of California, Davis; M.A., California State University, Sacramento; M.P.A., University of California, Riverside) is professor of marketing, College of Business Administration, California State University–Sacramento, where she teaches courses in consumer behavior and marketing research. Over her career she has received awards for outstanding teaching and distinguished service. She has published widely in a variety of journals, including *Journal of Advertising Research, Journal of Consumer Marketing, Journal of Services Marketing, Journal of Direct Marketing, Psychology and Marketing, Behavioral Science, Human Factors, Journal of Psychology, Applied and Basic Social Psychology, Journal of Education for Business,* and *Journal of College Student Development.* Her favorite consumers are her daughter, Stephanie, son, Ryan, and husband, Cal.

CONTENTS

GOLD NUGGETS

Take a jar, like a two-gallon pickle jar. First fill it to the top with gold nuggets. Then pour in as much gold dust as you can, filling up all the spaces between the gold nuggets.

Now dump everything out of the jar and separate the gold nuggets and the gold dust into two separate piles. Ok. Now, this time pour in all the gold dust first. Then put in all the gold nuggets. What happens is that the gold nuggets no longer fit.

It's best to put in the gold nuggets first. They are the most important. Then fill in the gaps with gold dust (i.e., the finer points and the details).

This is the idea behind this book. It isn't everything. It isn't all-inclusive. It is just the gold nuggets. Once you have collected the gold nuggets, it is much easier to fill the gaps with gold dust.

The jar holds so much more when you do it this way.

INTRODUCTION
UNDERSTANDING THE CONSUMER IS THE STARTING POINT.

REALITY IS WHATEVER THE CONSUMER SAYS IT IS

The Consumer's Reality: One Pound Is Not Always One Pound

The Consumer's Reality: Fifteen Dollars Is Not Always Fifteen Dollars

The Consumer's Reality: Half an Hour Is Not Always Half an Hour
Consumer Reality Is Not Always the Same as Objective Reality.

Product Failures: What Were They Thinking?

Product Successes: Consumer Classics

Product Successes: Consumer Fads
Successful Products Understand the Consumer. Begin by Understanding Your
Customer's Reality.

E-Commerce and the Consumer Connection: The Return of the Milkman
E-Commerce Makes the Need To Understand the Consumer Even More Important.

Cats Have Nine Lives
Products Can Have More Than One Life—The Rudolph Phenomenon.

*Marketing Reflects, Reinforces, Modifies, and Alters the Consumer's
Reality—But for the Better or Worse?*
Recognize the Power of Marketing To Shape Consumer Reality.

PERCEPTION
SEE THE WORLD THE WAY THE CONSUMER SEES THE WORLD.

UNDERSTANDING THE CONSUMER'S REALITY MEANS UNDERSTANDING HIS OR HER PERCEPTION

People See What They Expect To See
Consumer Expectations Influence Their Definitions of Reality.

Consumers Use Cues To Help Them Identify and Define Reality
Give Consumers the Cues To Perceive Your Product the Way You Want It To Be
Perceived.

What Is It? It's Obvious.
The Obvious Is Not Always Obvious. The Consumer's Perceptual Process Is Lightning
Quick.

Products Can Come To Own Cues
Cues Can Carve Out an Identity for the Product and Are Powerful Reminders and
Reinforcers.

Mixed Sensory Modalities
Consumers Taste with Their Eyes.
Consumers See with Their Noses.
A Sixth Sense: Your Nose Knows, Even if You Don't.

MOTIVATION
WHAT MAKES THE CONSUMER TICK?

INTRODUCTION

UNDERSTANDING THE CONSUMER IS THE STARTING POINT

REALITY IS WHATEVER THE CONSUMER SAYS IT IS

To successfully serve the consumers in your target market, you must first understand reality as your target market perceives it.

THE CONSUMER'S REALITY: ONE POUND IS NOT ALWAYS ONE POUND

When consumers are presented with two identical irons—one off-white and one black—and asked to pick up each one, examine each one, and then select the one that weighs more, consumers tend to indicate that the black iron weighs more. Objectively, each iron weighs the same. But that hardly matters. Consumers will tire more quickly using the black iron. Using the light-colored iron makes ironing a less onerous task for most consumers.

THE CONSUMER'S REALITY: FIFTEEN DOLLARS IS NOT ALWAYS FIFTEEN DOLLARS

A study asked consumers to answer the following question[1]: "Under which circumstance, Situation A or Situation B, would you be saving more?"

- ☐ Situation A: You are at **Nordstrom.** You see turtlenecks priced **"Everyday Low Price $15.00"**
- ☐ Situation B: You are at **Nordstrom.** You see turtlenecks priced **"Regularly $20.00/Sale $15.00"**

The study found that the majority of people select **Situation B** as the one in which they will save more money. Objectively, the consumer spends $15.00 in each situation. But it's not objective reality that matters—it's the **consumer's reality** that matters.

The same study presented the same two situations to another group of consumers and asked them to answer the following question: "Under which circumstance, Situation A or Situation B, do you feel you would be paying too much for a turtleneck?"

☐ Situation A: You are at **Nordstrom**. You see turtlenecks priced **"Everyday Low Price $15.00"**

☐ Situation B: You are at **Nordstrom**. You see turtlenecks priced **"Regularly $20.00/Sale $15.00"**

The study found that most people select **Situation A**. Once again, in objective reality the consumer spends $15.00 in each situation; however, in the consumer's reality the $15.00 in Situation A is not equal to the $15.00 in Situation B.

The Consumer's Reality: Half an Hour Is Not Always Half an Hour

Consumer reality is not always the same as objective reality.

Why is a half-hour wait at Disneyland so much shorter than a half-hour wait in line at the grocery store? Half an hour is not always half an hour. Half an hour spent in a line that keeps moving seems much shorter than half an hour spent in a line that doesn't move. It's not objective reality that matters. It's the consumer's experience that matters.

Product Failures: What Were They Thinking?[2]

Many failed products are testimonials to the lack of understanding of the consumer's reality.

In the early 1990s Planters introduced Planters Vacuum-Packed Peanuts. Consumers thought these vacuum-packed peanuts were bags of coffee beans. They poured them into the grocery stores' coffee bean grinders. They didn't get ground coffee—they got peanut butter and in the process gummed up and ruined the grinder machinery. The consumers were not happy, and store owners were not happy.

You may wonder how consumers could make such a mistake. Mr. Peanut was featured prominently on the package. The large-lettered label clearly stated that the contents were peanuts. This product was introduced, however, in the early 1990s, when vacuum-packed, flavored coffees such as hazelnut were also being introduced. In fact, Planters probably wanted to piggyback on the idea of "Fresh Roast" . . . fresh roast coffee—fresh roast[ed] peanuts. In the consumer's mind, coffee and hazelnut go together, coffee and chocolate go together, peanuts and chocolate go together, so it may not be that far-fetched to think that coffee and peanuts go together. In addition, the lack of uniformity in the size and shape of the peanuts produced lumpy packages that, combined with the lighting conditions in the stores, may have reduced the legibility of the labeling.

Nabisco's Baker Tom's Cat Food was different than other cat foods on the market because it was baked. The diagonal ribbon printed prominently across one corner of the package proudly declared it "The Only Baked Cat Food."

Consumers, however, did not really care how their cats' food was made, only that their cats ate it. Apparently cats had a hard time chewing Baker Tom's Cat Food and decided it wasn't worth eating. Consequently, repeat purchase was not sustained. That's what happens when you have a solution to a problem that consumers don't have.

People who smoke cigarettes enjoy the wreath of smoke that surrounds them. R. J. Reynolds invented a smokeless cigarette called Eclipse. This is a solution for nonsmokers who do not like cigarettes because of all the smoke that they produce. But who's buying the cigarettes? Not nonsmokers. This is what happens when you forget who your target market is.

PRODUCT SUCCESSES: CONSUMER CLASSICS

Consumer products such as Ivory Soap, Coca-Cola, Arm & Hammer Baking Soda, Quaker Oats, and Hershey's candy bars are part of the consumer landscape.

The Barbie doll has been a fixture in little girls' toy boxes for three generations and has added significant income to Mattel's bottom line. Introduced in 1959, the Barbie doll has been an incredibly successful toy. Ruth Handler, one of the founders of Mattel, captured the essence of the Barbie doll's success when she explained that "toys don't last, dreams do." The Barbie doll is the embodiment of America's dream girl. And as the American definition of femininity has changed over time, so has the Barbie doll. She has undergone over 40 facial variations (do we dare call them facelifts?), and her lifestyle accessories are like archeological fossils that record the changes in femininity in the United States since 1959. Barbie can be a babysitter, rock star, doctor, astronaut, beauty queen, presidential candidate—anything she wants. She has dozens of cars and motorcycles, owns over a dozen homes, and has well over 42 friends. When little girls play with Barbie, they can dream about their lives as adults.

The Barbie doll also has its detractors. Some wonder whether by playing with Barbie little girls are implicitly given a model of physical beauty that is impossible to attain. In fact, most little girls cannot grow up to be adults with Barbie-like measurements (38-18-34). Does Barbie teach little girls that success and happiness in adulthood come only to those who are beautiful? That material possessions are the key to happiness? Or is the Barbie doll just a toy, and these profound philosophical and psychological questions simply speculative?

PRODUCT SUCCESSES: CONSUMER FADS[3]

Not all products have to be long-lived to be successful, but they do have to be based on an understanding of the consumer. The Pet Rock came with a book of instructions on house-training: "Place it on some old newspapers. The rock will require no further instructions." The Pet Rock was easy to train. With a little help, it could roll over. Its best trick was playing dead. Gary Dahl sold 1.5 million Pet Rocks at $3.95 each ($11.25 in 1999 dollars). You do the math. Dahl laughed deliriously all the way to the bank.

Thirty-five years of Barbie.

In the early 1980s Harvard-trained Ken Hakuta, now known as "Dr. Fad," was exporting fish meal from the United States to his native Japan. One day Hakuta's children received a package from their grandmother in Japan—inside was a slimy, rubberlike, octopus-shaped toy. Thrown on the wall, the toy "walked" (with the help of gravity) all the way to the floor. Hakuta forked over $100,000 for the Wacky Wallwalker's North American distribution rights. He made more than $20 million.

Fads make an emotional connection with the whimsical needs of consumers. Whims are necessary and desirable fun. But whims are short-lived. The novelty wears off. Therefore, fads have to be constantly (re)invented. Currently the yo-yo's popularity is resurging. Can the resurrection of the Hula-Hoop be far off?

E-COMMERCE AND THE CONSUMER CONNECTION: THE RETURN OF THE MILKMAN[4,5]

"One-on-one marketing," "mass customization," "relationship marketing." Whatever you call it, technology is enhancing the ability of marketers to establish personalized service and relationships with individual customers.

British Airways installed a software system that tracks the beverage, food, reading, and other needs of its business-class and first-class patrons. Although this system allows British Airways to custom serve its most lucrative market segment, this system was originally installed to reduce inventory costs. *"You don't have to carry everything if you know what your customers want"* resulted in an estimated $5 to $8 million savings for British Airways.

The Ritz-Carlton uses CLASS (Customer Loyalty Anticipation Satisfaction System) technology to customize service to over 500,000 of its customers. Once a Ritz-Carlton employee learns that a customer has special requests—an extra-firm pillow, for example—this information is entered into the CLASS system. The next time that particular customer checks into a Ritz-Carlton hotel—*anywhere*—she will have an extra-firm pillow to caress and comfort her head. Like the Ritz-Carlton, Marriott International Inc. (which manages 1,850 hotels and resorts worldwide) uses customer-information software from Siebel Systems Inc. to track repeat-guest preferences, arming staff with the necessary information to cater to their customers' needs and provide them with the amenities they desire. E-commerce delivers with TLC.

Many people—especially women—prefer to try on clothes before they buy them, an option not available when buying clothes on the Internet. Lands' End, the mail order company known for its quality clothing—and renowned for its customer service—has come up with an alternative. The Lands' End web site allows female customers to build virtual models of themselves to try on garments. They can then select those garments that are most flattering to their figures and most complementary to their coloration.

Yahoo! allows visitors to establish personalized web pages, My Yahoo!, to serve individual information preferences. Dell Computer established a private web page for each of its high-volume customers. Flowers.com greets its customers by name, notifies them when products of potential interest become available, and even reminds them when it's time to plant, prune, or add vitamins and nutrients to their plants.

Ford Motor Company has launched an ambitious e-commerce plan to build cars with features specified by customers ordering from the Ford web site. Henry Ford, the founder of Ford Motor Co., told his customers they could have any color car they wanted as long as it was black. His great-grandson, Bill Ford, Jr., wants to be able to tell his customers that not only can they have any color they want, but that they can have any of a myriad of features.

Successful products understand the consumer. Begin by understanding your customer's reality.

The milkman developed relationships with his customers. He knew his customers by name, the amount and type of products they wanted, and he delivered right to their doors. E-Commerce has reinvented the milkman.

CATS HAVE NINE LIVES

Most people know the Christmas story of Rudolph, the Red-Nosed Reindeer. Rudolph was a misfit, shunned by all the other reindeer because he had a "very, very shiny nose." Then one foggy Christmas Eve, Santa needed Rudolph and his enormous red nose to guide his sleigh. Rudolph became a hero. Rudolph did not change. The environment changed. In one environment Rudolph was a misfit, the butt of jokes. In a changed environment Rudolph was transformed into a hero.

Most products go through a life cycle from introduction to growth to maturity to decline. Some products, such as Coca Cola, Hershey's, and Ivory Soap, have long life cycles, while other products, such as Rubik's Cube and the Pet Rock, have short life cycles. Amazingly some products come back from near death. Consider the story of Cheez Whiz. During the 1970s, it was a target of ridicule. It represented all things artificial. It was filler. Cheez Whiz was synonymous with things of questionable or marginal value. When the microwave oven came along, however, Cheez Whiz became wonderful. It was convenient. It was tasty. It was versatile. Cheez Whiz came back to life. Like Rudolph, some products shunned in one environment are valued in another.

MARKETING REFLECTS, REINFORCES, MODIFIES, AND ALTERS THE CONSUMER'S REALITY—BUT FOR THE BETTER OR WORSE?

Marketing interaction and communication with the consumer will alter, modify, and influence the consumer's reality. The advertisements shown below illustrate how *reality* has changed over time.

Cigarette smoking was once touted for its benefits. It was a digestion aid, a product recommended by doctors. It soothed the "T-zone." Today cigarettes are deemed sufficiently dangerous to mandate the printing of the surgeon general's warning on every package, and advertising on television is banned. Cigarette advertisements now proclaim that they have less tar and nicotine and are less dangerous.

It is doubtful that consumers today would eat a cake of yeast or mix a package of yeast into a drink. Why? Because yeast is a baking product. In the 1930s, however, yeast was consumed for medicinal purposes: to aid digestion, clear the skin of acne, and calm the nerves.

Today Listerine is a mouthwash. In the 1930s Listerine was used to treat dandruff.

It's hard to believe that Marlboro—the epitome of masculinity—was originally a pink-tipped cigarette designed for women.

New Parliament award for horsemanship? Neigh! The medallion's just a gentle reminder
that horsemen (like other smart Parliament smokers) want everyone to know *their cigarette* is special.
And you, too, will appreciate the crush-proof cigarette case . . . the superb tobaccos . . .
the luxurious flavor . . . and above all, the exclusive Mouthpiece that keeps the filter
deeply recessed away from your lips. With Parliaments, *only the flavor touches your lips!*

ONLY THE FLAVOR . TOUCHES YOUR LIPS

PERCEPTION

SEE THE WORLD THE WAY THE CONSUMER SEES THE WORLD

UNDERSTANDING THE CONSUMER'S REALITY MEANS UNDERSTANDING HIS OR HER PERCEPTION

Marketing begins with an understanding of the consumer's reality. All marketing efforts need to be carried out with a clear vision of the consumer's perception of reality. Marketing must identify those factors that influence the consumer's perception.

PEOPLE SEE WHAT THEY EXPECT TO SEE

WHICH IS THE PUTTY KNIFE? WHICH IS THE SANDWICH SPREADER?   Most people identify the utensil in picture A as the putty knife and the utensil in picture B as the sandwich spreader. In fact, it is the same utensil/tool in both pictures. But consumers have learned *to expect* to find a putty knife in a toolbox and a sandwich spreader in a kitchen drawer.

Picture A   Picture B

WHICH IS THE PAINTBRUSH? WHICH IS THE BASTING BRUSH? Most people identify the brush in picture A as the paintbrush and the brush in picture B as the basting brush. People expect to find paintbrushes among painting supplies and basting brushes in kitchen drawers.

Picture A

Picture B

Stare at picture A for about 45 seconds.

Picture A

Now stare at the picture B. What do you see?

Picture B

Most people look at picture B and see an old woman or a witch. Why? Because picture A primed you to expect to see the old woman/witch; consequently, when you looked at picture B you saw what you expected. In fact, picture B is a composite picture of both a witch and a young woman as illustrated in pictures C and D below.

Consumer expectations influence their definitions of reality.

Picture C

Picture D

Consumers Use Cues to Help Them Identify and Define Reality

Jiffy Blueberry Muffin Mix is a product found in the baking goods aisle in grocery stores. A picture of blueberry muffins dominates the package. The picture is juxtaposed with the words "Blueberry Muffin." Consumers buy the product, go home, and bake the blueberry muffins. They pour the contents of the package into a bowl, noting the flour-like mixture and the little round blueberries; they add an egg and some milk; they stir, pour, and bake. They can smell the aromatic muffins as they bake. In a few short minutes the muffins are ready, and after a few more minutes of cooling the muffins are consumed fresh. Delicious. Consumers will return to buy another package of Jiffy Blueberry Muffin Mix on subsequent grocery-shopping trips. End of story.

Let's rewind for a closer analysis. There are no blueberries in these "blueberry" muffins. However, there is absolutely nothing deceptive about the packaging. Clearly stated on the front of the package are the words "imitation blueberry" right next to the words "blueberry muffins." But the cues that capture the consumer's attention are the picture of the blueberry muffins and the word "blueberry," which is printed in blue type. Most consumers never see the word "imitation," even though it is right in front of their noses. Furthermore, when consumers make these blueberry muffins, they see the blueberries in the mix and can taste them when they eat the muffins. So what are those blueberries if they aren't real blueberries? Read the list of ingredients. Instead of blueberries, apples are used. The blueberries are little bits of apple dyed blue to look like blueberries and are flavored to taste like blueberries.

Give consumers the cues to perceive your product the way you want it to be perceived.

WHAT IS IT? IT'S OBVIOUS

In 1982 samples of Sunlight Dish Washing Detergent were distributed to households in the Northeast during the summer. To illustrate a key selling point of Sunlight—that it contained lemon juice—the package featured the words "real lemon juice" and a picture of a lemon. Thirty-three adults and 45 children thought the product was lemon juice, put it in their ice tea, drank it, and became ill enough to call a hospital or poison control hotline. How could this happen? Consumers zeroed in on the salient cues: the words "real lemon juice" and the picture of the lemon; consequently they identified the product as lemon juice. The fact that it was summer probably reinforced the perception that it was lemon juice.[1]

> The obvious is not always obvious. The consumer's perceptual process is lightning quick.

PRODUCTS CAN COME TO OWN CUES

Some marketers have deftly used cues to identify their products. What brand of soft drink comes to mind for each of the following colors?

☐ Red
☐ Blue
☐ Green

What brand of film comes to mind for each of the following colors?

☐ Green
☐ Yellow

> Cues can carve out an identity for the product and are powerful reinforcers and reminders.

For soft drinks, most people identify red as Coke, blue as Pepsi and green as 7-Up. For film, most people identify green as Fuji and yellow as Kodak.

MIXED SENSORY MODALITIES

A study asked consumers to taste three samples of chocolate pudding—dark brown, moderate brown, and light brown. Then the consumers were given a questionnaire that asked them to choose the pudding sample that was the richest tasting, the most chocolate tasting, the smoothest, and the creamiest. Consumers rated the dark brown pudding as the most chocolate tasting, and the richest tasting, and the light brown pudding as the creamiest. In fact, none of the pudding samples was chocolate pudding. All were vanilla pudding mixed with brown food coloring. Consumers tasted the pudding with their eyes.[2]

> Consumers taste with their eyes.

If you ask consumers how they determine the cleanliness of their clothes, they will tell you that they look at them. If you watch how consumers determine the cleanliness of their clothes, you will see that they not only look, they *smell*.

> Consumers see with their noses.

A little known organ in our nose, the vomero nasal organ (VNO), was thought to be a vestige of our evolutionary past, sort of like the appendix, with no apparent purpose or function. Recently, however, mounting evidence hints that the VNO is a receptor for pheromones, odorless chemical substances that may affect mood and sex states. It has been well known that nonhuman creatures in the animal kingdom communicate with and are affected by pheromones, but now it seems that humans may also unknowingly respond to these pollen-like chemicals. For example, pheromones have been suggested as the explanation for the menstrual synchrony phenomenon experienced by women who live together (e.g., mothers and daughters, female roommates). Perfume manufacturers such as Erox Corp. have been quick to incorporate pheromones in their product offerings: Realm for Men, Realm for Women and Inner Realm.[3,4]

A sixth sense: your nose knows, even if you don't.

ALL THE MARKETER'S CUES MUST COMMUNICATE THE SAME MESSAGE TO THE CONSUMER

The department store Target briefly carried pink-handled hammers. As you may have guessed, they did not sell well. Although a woman might consider buying this hammer, for men it's a hard sell. Pink just isn't an appropriate color for a man's toolbox. (Tim Taylor from the TV sitcom *Home Improvement* would not be caught dead with a pink hammer in his macho set of tools!) The hammer might be of good quality, but pink does not communicate strength.

Sending the consumer inconsistent cues not only dooms your product or service, it can make the consumer downright sick. Children who ate mashed potatoes dyed with blue food coloring became ill. Toro Corporation developed a lightweight, efficient snow thrower, named Snow Pup. Research undertaken to determine why sales lagged behind projections indicated that the name was at fault. Unfortunately, the name "Snow Pup" is inconsistent with the desired image of power. A pup is cute. It's cuddly. But it is not powerful. The product was renamed Snow Master and sales increased substantially. "Snow Master" is consistent with power and ability.

Packaging is an important cue. An ermine and a weasel are the same animal. In its winter white fur, it is an ermine. With its summer brown fur, it is a weasel. Ermines are perceived as exotic, high class, and smack of sophistication and elegance. Our everyday conversations often portray the weasel as despicable, conniving, underhanded, and not to be trusted: "Don't try to weasel out of this one!" and "You little weasel."

Giving tricky cues may be good in a game of murder whodunit, but it's not good for marketing your product to consumers. What is Thixo-Tex? You don't know. Neither did consumers. When the product was renamed Rusty Jones and launched with an advertising campaign, sales of the rust-proofing product went from $2 million to $100 million in 4 years.

McDonald's communicates cleanliness: clean tables, clean floors, clean counters, clean restrooms, and clean uniformed servers. McDonald's communicates efficiency. Cash registers are programmed so servers do not have to spend time entering multiple keystrokes for each item ordered. The server pushes a button on the soft drink machines preset for the chosen serving size. McDonald's communicates consistency. A Big Mac tastes the same at any McDonald's in the United

States. French fries taste the same whether they come from a McDonald's in Las Vegas or in Fargo, North Dakota. The ingredients and preparation methods are identical at all restaurants.[5-8]

THE JUST-NOTICEABLE DIFFERENCE (JND)

If you are on a diet and lose a couple of ounces, you don't consider it a victory in your quest to shed weight. In fact, it's more likely that you don't even notice the weight loss. You have to lose pounds to rightly claim that you have lost weight. Small differences are not noticeable. On the other hand, if you gain a couple of ounces, you don't even notice the weight gain, and you pat yourself on the back for not gaining weight.

Sometimes marketing strategies require that changes go unnoticed. Costs may require the manufacturer to charge more for the same amount of product. A way around the need to impose a price increase is to provide slightly less product for the same price. In this case, the manufacturer wants the change to go unnoticed. Consequently, products have been shrinking over the years, such as candy bars. Pizza Hut shrank its large pizza from 16 inches to 14 inches in 1995. The width of the seats on United Airlines airplanes has shrunk an inch or so. Scott has reduced the number of sheets of paper towels from 124 to 120 to 112 to 96, and Bounty had decreased its rolls from 80 to 72 to 64. Del Monte Pudding Cups have shrunk from 17 oz to 16 oz to 14 oz. This downsizing has been accomplished largely without the consumer's awareness.[9]

In other situations, the marketing strategy is for consumers to notice the change. Marketers who provide more product for the same price can raise awareness of the change by using signage, displays, and other attention-getting devices. Consumers, however, may not believe that there is a change unless the change is significant. Consumers will not believe that a product is on sale just because there is a sign declaring a sale. The change in price has to be sufficiently noticeable.

> Use cues to say it once, and say it again and again and again and again.

> Make JND the measurement of change.

REPEAT, REPEAT, REPEAT, *REPEAT*

The first time you saw it, it was captivating.
The second time you saw it, it was provocative.
The third time you saw it, it was arresting.
The fourth time you saw it, it was interesting.
The fifth time you saw it, you noticed it.
The sixth time you saw it, you really didn't pay attention.
The seventh time you saw it, you really didn't see it.

When you first walk into a seafood store, you may notice the seafood odor that pervades the air. After a few minutes in the store, however, you don't smell it anymore. People who live in high-rise apartments in urban areas don't really pay attention to or notice the muffled sirens that periodically scream by. When you first turn on your computer, you may notice the hum of the fan, but after a few minutes you don't really hear it anymore. Habituation or adaptation occurs when the stimulus—the seafood odor, the sound of the siren, or the hum of the fan, no

Changes in the Budweiser label over time.

longer captures attention. Marketers need to be aware of habituation and adaptation to prevent consumers from habituating/adapting to their advertisements.

CBS News has a Sunday-morning program aptly entitled *Sunday Morning. Sunday Morning* opens with a picture of the sun. Each segment closes with an illustration of the sun. Each of the suns is different. They have different expressions, different colors, different backgrounds. In letters to CBS, viewers express their enjoyment, surprise, and delight in seeing them.

GESTALTS

The Gestalt psychologists, guided by the principle that meaning is derived from a consideration of the totality of the stimulus and not from parts of the stimulus, discovered principles that guide perception. The principle of figure ground states that people perceive the figure against the background. When consumers see an ad, they perceive the advertised product against the background. If consumers cannot tell which is the figure and which is the background, they will work at it

Black brings out the brilliance of the holidays.

Ultimately, there's Black.™

In this ad for Johnny Walker Scotch, consumers do not see a string of lights—they see the pattern, a decorated Christmas tree.

until they do. In this advertisement for Absolut Vodka, consumers have to distin-guish the Absolut Vodka bottle from its background.

The principle of closure suggests that consumers close gaps to perceive the whole. Consumers do not see isolated bits and pieces. Rather, they tend to fill in the gaps to perceive the whole pattern.

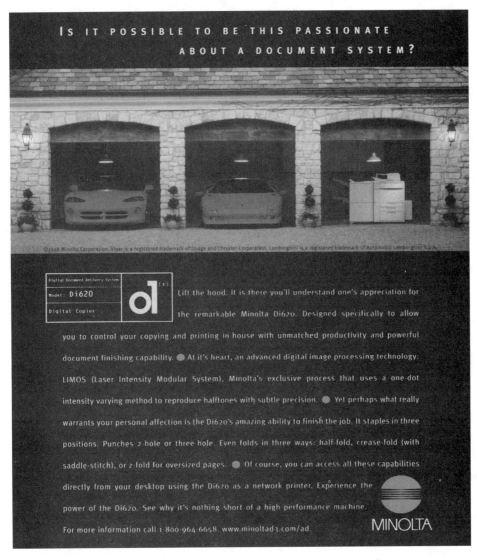

The Minolta Copier is so valuable that, like an automobile, it should have its own garage.

The principle of similarity indicates similar things are perceived as a group. Consumers tend to group similar objects as belonging together.

The principle of common fate states that people see things going in the same direction as belonging together.

Perception is holistic: "The whole is more than the sum of its parts."

Proud to be
a sponsor of the
U.S. Ski Team.

Chevy Trucks
LIKE A ROCK

All the other cars have the common fate of being stuck in the snow. The Chevy Truck is
the only one that can operate under these demanding environmental conditions.

SUBLIMINAL ADVERTISING

*What you see is
what you get . . .
maybe.*

Subliminal advertising contains elements presented below the consumer's conscious level of awareness. Controversy swirls around its existence and effective-
ness. It is a subject that waxes and wanes in the media but refuses to go away. It
raises a host of questions with no definitive answers: Do subliminal ads communicate with the unconscious? Are subliminal ads more effective because they by-
pass the consumer's conscious censorship? Are subliminal advertisements like
looking at steam, smoke, or clouds (i.e., you can see whatever you want)? Is the
whole subject of subliminal advertising a publicity stunt to get consumers to look
at advertisements?

subliminal advertising experiment

fcuk™
New York London

This advertisement is poking fun at subliminal advertisements.

"Today I met with a subliminal advertising executive for just a second."
—Steven Wright.

BRANDS TAKE ON THE CHARACTERISTICS OF THE PRODUCT CATEGORY

Consumers who find Sunkist Fruit Gems, a soft, fruit-flavored candy-like product, among the apples, oranges, bananas, and other fruits in the grocery store are likely to see them as healthy and nutritious. Consumers who find Sunkist Fruit Gems in the candy section of the grocery store are likely to think of them as candy: tasty and fun to eat, but not nutritious.

If Mrs. Dash seasoning is a spice you would put it in the spice rack and use it when cooking. If Mrs. Dash is a salt substitute, you would put it on the table and use it when eating.

If Snickers is a nutritious snack chock-full of peanuts, then you could eat it guilt free between meals. If Snickers is a candy bar, you might hesitate to eat it.

After two decades and several million dollars, J.C. Penney admitted its attempt to reposition itself as an upscale department store was not going to be accepted by

> Position your
> brand in the
> right category.

Is this more than just an advertisement for Tabasco sauce?

consumers. To consumers, J.C. Penney is a mass merchandiser that supplies Middle America with everyday needs at sensible prices.[8] Montgomery Ward tried to sell fur coats. It didn't work because Montgomery Ward does not fit the category of stores selling fur coats.

WALK LIKE YOUR CONSUMER. SHOP LIKE YOUR CONSUMER. BUY LIKE YOUR CONSUMER.

The United States is a right-handed, right-direction country. Americans drive on the right side of the road. They walk on the right side of the sidewalk. They enter revolving doors on the right and make them go counterclockwise. They cut their meat with their right hand and transfer the fork to the right hand. So naturally Americans go right when they walk into stores. Consumers would head toward high-profit goods if they were placed on the right.

Americans read from left to right. Consumers would see new brands if placed on the shelf to the right of the old established brand.

Consumers walk into the store and don't bother to get a basket because they are only picking up a few things. Once they start strolling the aisles, they find themselves picking up much more than they came in for, and their hands are getting full. They want to buy more, but they don't have a basket. It would be smart for the marketer to place baskets strategically throughout the store.

Consumers walk into the store, pick up a cart and quickly fill up the cart. They need more things, but the cart is full. They would buy more if they had a bigger cart.

Cosmetic displays capture the consumer's attention. She stops to examine the products. The display is set up in a small space and people keep brushing her backside as they pass. She stops examining the cosmetics and moves on. This is known as the "butt-brush" factor.[10] Women hate to be jostled from behind. She might have stayed and purchased a few items if she had had a bit more room.

When the line at the checkout stand is incredibly long, consumers will abandon full carts. The wait would seem so much shorter if they had something to do, such as reading. When the consumer is on hold for so long she feels like she will expire before anyone talks to her she hangs up the phone. She would have waited longer had she been told approximately how much longer she would have to wait, how many callers were ahead of her, or had been given a choice of musical selections to listen to while she waited.[11,12]

Get rid of the weeds in the consumer's path.

MOTIVATION

WHAT MAKES THE CONSUMER TICK?

NEEDS AND OPPORTUNITIES MOTIVATE CONSUMERS

When consumers ask to try on a pair of shoes at Nordstrom's Department Store, the sales reps bring a pair in the requested size and in sizes just larger and smaller. The service clerks at Raley's Bel Air Supermarket, located in northern California, bag their customers' groceries and help load the groceries in their customers' cars. At South City Honda in Sacramento, California, customers receive a free car wash with any servicing or oil change. Customers can also avail themselves of the free shuttle that will drop them off at home or work and will pick them up when the servicing is complete. Women's Work is a professional group of painters (all women) who have differentiated themselves by cleaning up, vacuuming, and returning furniture to its original location after they are finished painting.

> You satisfice needs. You optimize opportunities.

When an optometrist fits a consumer for glasses, he or she typically asks the consumer to indicate which pair of lenses works best: "Which was better, the first or the second?" The optometrist wants the best vision for the consumer, not an okay vision or even a better vision, but the best vision.

FROM HIGH INVOLVEMENT DECISION MAKING TO LOW INVOLVEMENT DECISION MAKING

The level of motivation results in different types of consumer behavior. High levels of motivation result in high involvement decision making, and low levels of motivation result in low involvement decision making. Some decisions, such as what college to attend, whom to marry, whether to marry, or what house to purchase, are important, involving decisions. Other decisions, such as what socks to wear today or what to buy for dessert at the grocery store, are not important and not involving decisions.

TABLE 3.1	DO YOU KNOW THE PRODUCTS BEING ADVERTISED BY THESE JINGLES?

1. Be all that you can be.
2. Good to the last drop.
3. The Quicker-Picker-Upper
4. The nighttime, sniffling, sneezing, coughing, aching, stuffy head, so-you-can-rest medicine.
5. Don't leave home without it.
6. Ring around the collar
7. Breakfast of champions
8. Where's the beef?
9. Please, don't squeeze the _____!
10. In the Valley of the Jolly ["Ho, Ho, Ho"] _____.
11. Mmmmmmmmmm Mmmmmmmmmmm Good!
12. The milk chocolate that melts in your mouth—not in your hand.
13. Look, Mom, no cavities!
14. They're Gr-r-reat!
15. Snap, crackle, pop
16. My bologna has a first name, it's _____.

ANSWERS: 1. U.S. Army, 2. Maxwell House Coffee, 3. Bounty paper towels, 4. NyQuil, 5. American Express, 6. Wisk, 7. Wheaties, 8. Wendy's, 9. Charmin toilet paper, 10. Green Giant, 11. Campbell's Soup, 12. M&Ms, 13. Crest Toothpaste, 14. Kellogg's Frosted Flakes, 15. Rice Krispies, 16. O-s-c-a-r (Oscar Mayer).

High involvement and low involvement decision making differ in important ways. The type and amount of information and the process of gathering product information differ.

It is highly unlikely that you purposely and intentionally learned the jingles listed in Table 3.1. However, it is highly likely that you were able to identify the products associated with the jingles. Most likely you learned them in a passive, haphazard, unintentional, nonpurposeful state of mind. In the same manner, you learned product and company logos—the swoosh (Nike), the golden arches (McDonald's), the cowboy (Marlboro), and the peacock (NBC). You could easily pick out the Gerber baby from a lineup.

Consumers' knowledge of logos and jingles shows how they obtain information for **low involvement decision making.** Under such circumstances, the decision just isn't very important to them, and the level of motivation is low. They do not make much effort or spend much time evaluating critically the alternatives available. Under low involvement consumers learn about brands in a passive, haphazard, unintentional, unfocused manner via repetitive, attention-getting advertisements and promotions. This is most likely how consumers learned the product logos and jingles mentioned above. It's unlikely that many consumers

Stock	Div	Sls hds	Lst Trn	Net Chg
DataRet n		5667	30.63	+1.62
DataSyst		94	4.69	+.12
Datalink n		195	14.81	+.43
Dataram s		8539	u30.56	−2.44
Datascpe	.16	678	38.38	−.86
Datastr		3935	9.19	+.42
Dataware		425	4.69	−.27
Dtawtch		284	2.00	

PENTIUM II 366 MHz
system, 64 meg SDRAM, 6.5 gig hdd, 24x cdrom, voo-doo graphics, 17 in svga mon., sound, speakers, kb, mouse, modem, win 95 or 98. $825/ofr. Mike (314) 576-4296

FRIENDS FIRST
Attractive, DWM, 40, 6'3", 205 lb, romantic-at-heart, loves sports, camping, Metro area, quiet dinners. Seeking S/DWF, 28-38, N/S, N/D, down-to-earth type, similar interests. Let's take time to be friends first. ☎ 5555

The abbreviated, shortened, compressed format of stock listings and classified ads does not deter the motivated, highly involved consumer.

sat down one day and purposefully, intentionally, and actively memorized logos and jingles.

For low involvement products, marketers must capture the consumer's attention for a sufficient length of time for them to learn the brand name of the product and its purpose. To be effective, the communication should include some element(s) to increase memorability, such as the use of logos, jingles, and well-known personalities; in addition, it should be repetitive so that the product remains in the forefront of the consumer's mind. However, to prevent "wear-out," it's normally best to consider restating a theme.

The stock listings, the classified ad offering a computer for sale, and the want ad for companionship are set in very small print. They abbreviate, shorten, and compress at the expense of clarity. You really have to focus your attention to read the ads. You probably read want ads only when you really need the information. The average consumer does not read the classifieds and stock listings on a daily basis.

When a consumer's motivation is high, he or she is **highly involved** in the decision-making process and spends considerable time, energy, and effort to evaluate and choose the alternative that is the most likely to satisfy his or her need. Marketers need to understand that these are not trivial decisions but ones that consumers take seriously. Under such circumstances, consumers want meaningful information. Consumers will seek out, read, and evaluate information about the products.

High involvement decision making is "Think before you act."
Low involvement decision making is "Act before you think."

OUT OF SIGHT, OUT OF MIND

When was the last time you went to a grocery store asking for a new candy bar or a new soft drink you saw in a television commercial? Never.

Prominent shelf space is imperative for selling low involvement products. Consumers must see them to consider buying them. A primo shelf location at eye level or at the end of an aisle or close to the checkout stands is highly coveted. Money spent for promotional displays to gain visibility is normally a good investment.

Retailers are not as interested in carrying particular brands as they are in profit per linear foot of shelf space. Armed with up-to-the-minute UPC data, retailers can track the movement and profitability of brands currently in their stores. Given that the proliferation of new brands is growing much faster than the availability of shelf space, the stage is set for confrontations between suppliers and retailers. Retailers have the more advantageous position. In fact, it is a common practice among grocery stores to ask/suggest/demand that manufacturers pay "slotting fees" to have their products occupy shelf space. This practice of charging tens of thousands of dollars in slotting fees (per brand) has made shelf space extremely expensive real estate.

> Shelf space: the most expensive real estate in town.

TWO-FACED PEOPLE NEED TWO-BRAINED COMMUNICATIONS

People may think of themselves as symmetrical. After all, human beings have two legs, two arms, two eyes. If we fold ourselves in half vertically from head to toe, we would match. But in reality, people are not symmetrical. People are really two-faced. On page 29 are composite pictures of two right halves and two left halves of people's faces. If people were symmetrical, you really couldn't tell their composite left face from their composite right face. But as the pictures show, people are not symmetrical. This is true of brainy people like Bill Gates and beautiful people like Cindy Crawford.

Consumers don't *think* symmetrically either. The right half of the human brain is adept at processing information sequentially, whereas the left brain is skilled at processing information simultaneously. The left brain specializes in verbal and logical functions. The right brain is skilled in intuitive, creative, and pictorial operations.

Recognize that some products are predominately left-brain products and others are right-brain products. Right-brain products are buy-before-you-think products. Consumers don't care too much about these products: candy bars, toilet tissue, shoelaces, canned peaches. Marketers need not bother wasting their time and money telling consumers about candy bars. Consumers don't want to know. Marketers need only to tell them the vitals: brand name, package, and one or two selling points—rich, creamy chocolate and melt-in-your-mouth buttery caramel. Television commercials are an effective way to communicate right-brain information to consumers, and the use of music, logos, jingles, spokespersons, and novelty will help plant the information in the consumer's memory.

Two-faced Bill Gates.

Two-faced Cindy Crawford.

Left-brain products are think-before-you-buy products. Consumers care about these products: cars, computers, dress shoes. Marketers need to provide consumers with information about their products. Consumers want to know. Therefore make sure the sales reps are knowledgeable and well trained. Budget for print ads and brochures.

FEELING PRODUCTS/THINKING PRODUCTS

If you visit the greeting card department of a grocery store or drug store the day before Mother's Day, you will find the area in front of the greeting cards clogged with consumers reading cards, trying to find just the right card to express their feelings for their mother. Greeting cards are feeling products.

Consumers may think of computers as an extension of themselves. However, most consumers would not conceive of computers as extensions of their heart. Rather, computers are extensions of their mind, their brain, their ability to think. Computers are thinking products.

	Thinking Products	Feeling Products
High Involvement	IRA account 35 mm camera Car battery	Car Wallpaper Perfume
Low Involvement	Insecticide Clothes pins	Greeting cards Ice cream Rum

The advertising agency Foote, Cone & Belding has developed a classification grid for products that is instrumental in helping marketers understand how their target market perceives their product. The grid classifies products as *thinking* or *feeling* and as *high involvement* or *low involvement*.[1,2]

MOTIVATIONAL RESEARCH TECHNIQUES ARE SHOVELS, NOT RAKES

Motivational research techniques provide consumers with methods to express themselves and their feelings about products in ways that may complement the survey technique. Consumers may be asked to draw pictures of users of a product, draw pictures to express their feelings toward a product, tell a story about a picture involving the product shown, or write an obituary about a product.

Whereas social norms and etiquette may influence and dictate the proper or socially acceptable responses consumers feel they should offer in interviews or surveys, motivational techniques are designed to dig beneath the consumers' socialized surface layers. These techniques can perhaps reveal motivational forces not readily evident on the surface.

Consumers were asked to draw pictures of the woman who uses Duncan Hines and the woman who used Pillsbury. The drawings revealed not only that

Negative space is defining something by what it is not. It is all the space that surrounds the object. If you define all the space around the object, you indirectly define the object.

Picture A shows a vase and two faces. The vase is the object. The two faces is the negative space around the vase. Picture B shows one half of the picture. You can think of it as one-half of the vase or as one of the two faces. Use Picture B to complete the picture by concentrating or focusing on the vase, which is the object. Drawing the vase would be a right-brain approach. Drawing the "opposite" face to the one shown in Picture B is a left-brain approach and is more difficult.

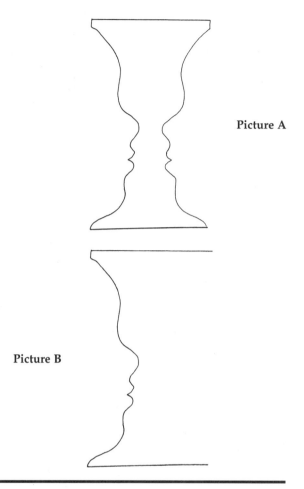

Picture A

Picture B

consumers view the Duncan Hines woman as contemporary and the Pillsbury woman as traditional, but how they actually visualized them.[4]

Women drew pictures of the way they felt about roaches and insecticides. These pictures showed that these women viewed roaches as the men in their lives who abandoned them. These women preferred spray insecticides that allowed them to witness the death-throes of the roaches to products that did not allow them to see the roaches die. For these women, killing roaches provided a vicarious emotional release to avenge themselves against the men in their lives who had done them wrong.[5] Motivational research was able to reveal reason for consumers' underlying psychological need for spray insecticides. It is doubtful that survey research would have uncovered this finding.

Digging a little deeper may reveal true motivations in consumer behavior.

How consumers view Duncan Hines and Pillsbury customers.

The Mind of a Roach Killer

The McCann-Erickson ad agency asked women to draw and describe how they felt about roaches. The agency concluded from the drawings that the women identified the roaches with men who had abandoned them and thus enjoyed watching the roaches-men squirm and die. That's why, the agency figured, that women prefer spray roach killers to products that don't allow the user to see the roach die.

"ONE NIGHT I just couldn't take the horror of these bugs sneaking around in the dark. They are always crawling when you can't see them. I had to do something. I thought wouldn't it be wonderful if when I switched on the light the roaches would shrink up and die like vampires to sunlight. So I did, but they just all scattered. But I was ready with my spray so it wasn't a total loss. I got quite a few...continued tomorrow night when night time falls."

"I TIPTOED quietly into the kitchen perhaps he wasn't around. I stretched my arm up to the light. I hoped I'd be alone when the light went on. Perhaps he is sitting on the table I thought. You think that's impossible? Nothing is impossible with that guy. He might not even be alone. He'll run when the light goes on I thought. But what's worse is for him to slip out of sight. No, it would be better to confront him before he takes control and 'invites a companion'."

"A MAN LIKES a free meal you cook for him, as long as there is food he will stay."

The mind of a roach killer.

THE PERENNIAL PROBLEM: NOT ENOUGH TIME AND NOT ENOUGH MONEY

Motivational conflict is a problem that all too often confronts consumers when they have multiple needs but insufficient funds and/or time to satisfy all the needs.

Marketing strategy should include recognizing motivational conflict and then providing the product or service as the solution to the problem.

Approach–avoidance motivational conflict occurs when the consumer's behavior has both a negative and positive consequence.

It's Thanksgiving dinner and the whole extended family is there—all 30 of you. The ovens, stovetops and outdoor grills have been going non-stop all day. The

Example of a solution to the approach–avoidance motivational conflict of overindulging.

turkey is the centerpiece! There is mashed potatoes with gravy, baked sweet pota-toes, bread stuffing and rice stuffing, cranberries with orange, cranberries with nuts, three vegetable dishes, apple pie, pumpkin pie, lemon meringue, and of course ice cream. And yes, Aunt Mable made two types of home-made bread—wheat bread and potato bread. Not to offend any of the cooks or to show fa-voritism, you do your part and eat one helping of each of the bountiful offerings. Consumers love to overindulge (positive/approach) but dislike the negative con-sequences of heartburn and indigestion (avoidance) it produces. Pepto Bismol po-sitions itself as the solution.

Students sometimes find themselves in a common approach–avoidance moti-vational conflict situation. Students may find that they have to or want to miss class (approach), but they do not want to miss lecture notes (avoidance). Students have initiated innovative solutions to this problem (e.g., establishing web sites that provide free lecture notes). Online lecture notes are a student solution for a student problem.

Approach–approach motivational conflict arises in those situations in which con-sumers have more than one need that clamors for satisfaction; however, limita-tions prevent consumers from satisfying all their needs.

Consumers may want to buy *both* a CD player (approach) *and* a new pair of shoes (approach), but only have enough cash for one item. They do not want to wait. They want the items right now. Credit card companies position themselves as the solution for instant gratification. Consumers can have both the CD player and a new pair of shoes right now.

In an approach–approach situation, consumers want it all and they want it now. They do not want to choose. They do not want to compromise. Consumers do not want an *either/or* solution. Consumers want a *both/and* solution. Roper Re-search has dubbed this the "cool fusion solution." This may explain the popular-ity of SUVs (sport utility vehicles), which provide consumers with *both* fun *and* function; casual dress that allows consumers to be *both* comfortable *and* profes-sional in appearance; and premium store brands that offer *both* quality *and value*.

In the *avoidance–avoidance motivational conflict* consumers are caught between a rock and a hard place. They are faced with having to choose between two alter-natives, both of which have negative consequences. This is illustrated in the ad-vertisement for Blue Cross/Blue Shield. The consumer does not want to choose the door on the right (avoidance), nor does he want to choose the door on the left (avoidance). Solution: choose the lesser of two evils.

Contemporary appliances and services were invented as solutions to consumer avoidance–avoidance motivational conflict. Consumers do not want to clean their ovens (avoidance). It is such an unpleasant chore. But consumers do not want to bake cookies and cakes or roast chicken and beef in a dirty oven (avoidance). It causes such an unpleasant odor. The self-cleaning oven is the solution to the con-sumer avoidance–avoidance motivational conflict.

Most consumers do not want to wear glasses (avoidance). Glasses are uncom-fortable, cause permanent indentations on the bridge of the nose, and require frequent cleanings. Contact lenses demand constant attention (avoidance). Con-sumers must buy contact lens solutions, clean the lenses, and monitor the amount

Approach–avoidance: how not to have to pay for what you want.

Approach–approach: how to have your cake and eat it, too.

It is no easy task to control costs and still manage to keep employees happy with their health benefits. Especially when you have employees in more than one state. But that's exactly what we're prepared to help you do—and better than anyone else.

The reason lies in a simple fact. No one knows local providers—how to evaluate them, to negotiate with them, to manage relationships with them—the way we do. Our local Plans are the most experienced provider contracting organizations in the business. They are there to manage the networks after they are established. That's why we can reduce costs while offering your employees the best selection of doctors and hospitals.

Not only do we manage HMOs and PPOs in over 200 cities, but through HMO-USA™ and Preferred Care-USA™ we bring them together into a consolidated national program to meet multi-state employer needs.

You get one account coordinator and consolidated billing, collection and disbursement through a single point. And our Away From Home Care program makes it easy for travelling employees to get care wherever they are.

Custom Care-USA™—our utilization review program—is built on a strong set of performance standards and the resources to back them up. Like 1200 nurse reviewers and over 1000 physician consultants. And an Individual Case Management Network, offering you on-site supervision of high cost cases by local case managers across the country.

These are some of the reasons our managed care programs serve over 30 million people. If you'd like more information, call 1-800-426-2583. We'll help you open the door to a few more options.

Blue Cross. Blue Shield.

Example of avoidance–avoidance motivational conflict.

of time they wear them. Consumers put up with glasses and contact lenses because they do not want to stumble through life like Mr. Magoo, the affable, visually impaired cartoon character (avoidance). Solution: Laser eye surgery that will restore the consumer's vision to 20/20 or better. No more glasses. No more contact lenses. No more Mr. Magoo.

To solve the mystery of the genetic code, Watson and Crick had to untangle the double helix. To solve avoidance–avoidance motivational conflicts, marketers must untangle double trouble.

CLASSIFICATION OF NEEDS

An accurate watch provides consumers with security—they know that they will be on time to work and other important appointments. An expensive watch is a mark of achievement. A watch given as a birthday present conveys love. A watch can be many things, serve many functions, convey many meanings for consumers.

The research of Abraham Maslow suggests that consumers' needs and motives are hierarchically ordered. Motives and needs lower on the hierarchy must be satisfied before higher-level needs and motives become activated, requiring satisfaction.

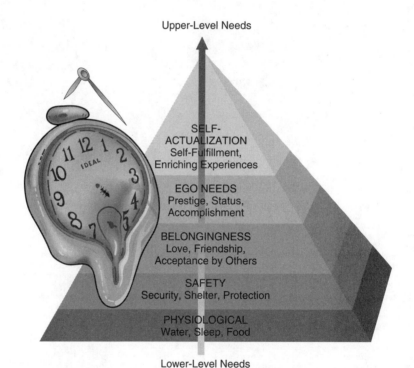

Maslow's hierarchy of needs.

LEARNING AND MEMORY

I CAN'T GET THAT SONG OUT OF MY HEAD

CLASSICAL CONDITIONING, HYPERTEXT, AND NEURAL LINKAGES

Those familiar with the Internet are familiar with hypertext—those highlighted words, pictures, and symbols that with a click of the mouse instantaneously link you to web sites of interest. This is classical conditioning—linkages among things. If you are the Coca-Cola Company, you want Coke to be linked with positive thoughts, feelings, and memories: fun, great taste, and refreshment. These associations are established through a type of learning called *classical conditioning.*

The Coca-Cola Company understands classical conditioning. It has taught the American people to love Coke. How else can you explain the massive public outcry in April 1985 when the original formula was replaced with New Coke? Coca-Cola received 1500 phone calls daily from consumers, pleading for the return of Classic Coke. The 6-o'clock news was filled with stories about people, including celebrities, hoarding Coke. Three months later, Coca-Cola Classic returned to the market.

Classical conditioning can explain how people learned to love Coke. Over the years, Coca-Cola developed advertisements, sponsored events, and offered promotions that juxtaposed Coke with positive events, happy times, and refreshing, uplifting, pleasant situations. In addition, classical conditioning can explain the positive images, thoughts, and feelings that come to mind when consumers see the Nike swoosh and McDonald's golden arches.

When Carolyn Davidson, a graduate of Portland State University, Oregon, designed the Nike swoosh (for thirty-five dollars) for Nike CEO Phil Knight, the world had not yet heard of Nike. The swoosh symbol had no meaning. Since then, the pairing of the Nike symbol with the aerodynamics of gravity-defying Michael Jordan has imparted to the Nike symbol the meanings and feelings consumers have toward Michael Jordan. Over time, the Nike commercials have expanded to include other renowned athletes. For many consumers, the Nike swoosh is synonymous with excellence in athletics.[1]

Through its many commercials, event sponsorships, and community involvement, McDonald's has conditioned consumers to associate the golden arches with good-tasting food, convenience, fun, and friends. Consider how often consumers are exposed to the golden arches on a typical visit. First, customers are greeted by the golden arches upon entering the restaurant—on the menu and on the servers' uniforms. As consumers eat their meals, they are exposed to the golden arches on the packaging—cups, wrappers, coffee stirrers, napkins, trays—and the decor. Finally, as consumers leave the restaurant, the two-story Golden Arches monument on the parking lot bids them adieu.

Associations give images and feelings to products.

For marketers, classical conditioning requires that they carefully choose events, persons, and objects to pair with their brands so that the right meanings and feelings rub off on consumers.

These pairings should be repetitive and frequent over time to be effective. Classical conditioning is more likely to occur under low involvement situations (see page 26, Chapter 3: Motivation).

"ME TOO" PACKAGING

Store brands, which are placed right next to the national brands on the shelf, are purposely packaged to look quite similar to the national brands. Marketers design store-brand packaging to be similar in shape, size, design, and colors. Retailers like the strategy. The store brands can piggyback (at little cost) on the advertising and hard-won identity, feelings, and knowledge that consumers have developed for the national brand. Retailers hope that the meanings and feelings consumers have for the national brands will *generalize* to the economically priced store brands.

Judge a book by its cover.

Oreos, Fig Newtons, and Chips Ahoy cookies carry the Nabisco family name. Hammers, saws, and wrenches from Sears carry the brand name Craftsman. Many products from Kraft, including gelatin, pudding, and no-bake desserts, carry the family name Jell-O. Nabisco wants consumers to recognize that all Nabisco cookies are fresh, delicious, and satisfying. Sears wants consumers to know that all Craftsman tools are high quality, professional, durable, and long lasting. Kraft wants consumers to know that all the desserts bearing the Jell-O family name taste good and are fun to eat.

There is a family resemblance.

A product family name uses the classical conditioning principle of stimulus generalization. People generalize the feelings and thoughts about all the products with the same family name.

Generalization has its limitations and marketers need to recognize when it should not be used. Maalox introduced an over-the-counter indigestion medication in whipped cream form. Efficol had the same idea and created a whipped cream cough medicine called Cough Whip. But whipped cream is something you put on desserts like Jell-O, pumpkin pie, and banana splits. Consumers look forward to whipped cream. It's a rich, sweet indulgence. Medicine tastes yucky and is something you have to take. Offering medicine in whipped-cream form to make it more palatable and easier to use does not work, and consumers did not buy it.[3]

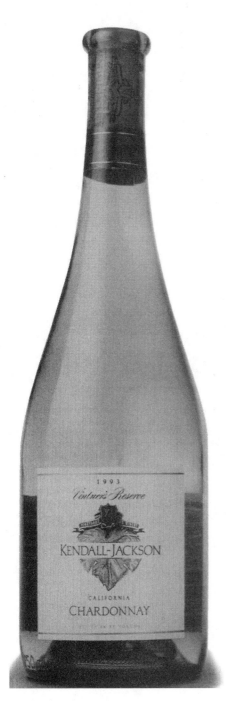

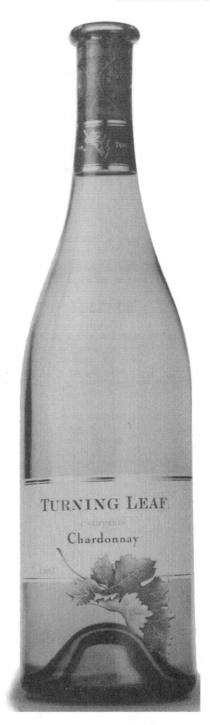

Consider these two products. They look remarkably alike. Officials at Kendall-Jackson believed that the packaging for Gallo's chardonnay was too similar to its own and brought suit. (Kendall-Jackson lost.)

How similar are these two logos? Too similar, according to officials at GoTo.com, an Internet search engine company that sued the Disney Go Network. (Disney lost.)

Imitation may not always be the sincerest form of flattery.

Lacoste is not crying crocodile tears. The French maker of the crocodile-logo polo shirt is crying foul at the Hong Kong retailer's logo. Lacoste thinks the Crocodile logo too closely resembles its crocodile logo.[2]

The clear-product trend of the early 1990s witnessed the introduction of a plethora of "clear" products such as Clearly Canadian, a sweetened sparkling water; clear Windex window cleaner; and clear Ivory dishwashing detergent. Not to be left out, Pepsi spent $100 million to introduce Crystal Pepsi, which failed. To consumers, Pepsi is brown, not clear. A clear, colorless beverage does not fit the image of the Pepsi family brand name.[3-5]

Generalization has its limitations.

THE DIFFERENCE THAT COUNTS

The flip side of stimulus generalization is stimulus discrimination. Whereas stimulus generalization is about similarity, stimulus discrimination is about differences. Marketing efforts based on stimulus generalization emphasize similarities. In contrast, marketing efforts based on stimulus discrimination emphasize a product's differences—the features that make the product better than its competitors.

Discrimination: It can be politically correct.

Same. Same. Same. Same. Same. Same. Same. Same.
Same. Same. Same. Same. Same. Same. Same. Same.
Same. Same. Same. Same. Same. Same. Same. Same.
Same. Same. Same. Same. Same. Same. Same. Same.
Same. Same. Same. Same. Same. Same. Same. Same.
Same. Same. Same. Same. Same. Same. Same. Same.
Same. Same. Same. Same. Same. Same. Same. Same.
Same. Same. Same. Same. Same. Same. Same. Same.
Same. Same. Same. Same. Same. Same. Same. Same.
Same. Same. Same. Same. Same. Same. Same. Same.
Same. Same. Same. Same. Same. Same. Same. Same.
Same. Same. Same. Same. Same. Same. Same. Same.
Same. Same. Same. Same. Same. Same. Same. Same.
Same. Same. Same. Same. Same. Same. Same. Same.
Same. Same. Same. Same. Same. Same. Same. Same.
Same. Same. Same. Same. Same. Same. Same. Same.
Same. Same. Same. Same. Same. Same. Same. Same.
Same. Same. Same. Same. Same. Same. Same. Same.
Same. Same. Same. Same. Same. Same. Same. Same.
Same. Same. Same. Same. Same. Same. Same. Same.
Same. Same. Same. Same. Same. Same. Same. Same.
Same. Same. Same. Same. Same. Dodge 🐏 Different.

Among the many brands of cars on the market, Dodge wants consumers to see that all the other cars are similar to each other, and Dodge is different.

OPERANT CONDITIONING

TRY IT—YOU MIGHT LIKE IT

Operant conditioning is trial-and-error learning. It is a type of learning initiated by the consumer's behavior, which results in a consequence. If the consequence is positive, then the consumer is likely to engage in the behavior in the future. On the other hand, if the consequence is negative, then the probability that the consumer will engage in the behavior in the future decreases.

The message to marketers from operant conditioning is straightforward. Make the consequence of the consumer's behavior pleasant and rewarding. The probability of repeat consumer behavior increases if marketers provide consumers with a quality product delivered with quality service.

Sees Candy is a successful candy store. Consumers purchase Sees Candy to give away on special occasions such as Mother's Day, Christmas, Valentines Day, Thanksgiving, birthdays, graduation, and as thank-you gifts. In addition, consumers buy Sees Candy for themselves for no particular reason. Sees Candy stores have a very simple color scheme—white. The employees wear white uniforms. The store walls are white. The stores are small, with just enough room for a candy counter where customers can custom-select individual chocolates. Preboxed assortments are also available. Every customer who buys candy from Sees is given a free piece of chocolate candy served in a brown candy cup. Even if all you buy is a thirty-five-cent Sees lollipop, you and everyone in your party will be offered a sample of chocolate candy.

> Strive to make the consequence of every consumer experience a positive one.

SOMETIMES IT'S A GOOD IDEA TO KICK-START CONSUMERS INTO ACTION

Every Wednesday the *Sacramento Bee* includes supermarket supplements that feature items on sale. During basketball season, Sacramento department stores such as JC Penney announce that members of the Sacramento Kings basketball team will be in the store to autograph photographs and souvenirs. Macy's department store announces that with every $25 Estee Lauder purchase, consumers will be given a gift pack (valued at $35) that is crammed full with lipstick, eye shadow, comb, perfume samples, night-time rejuvenating cream, and lotion. These events are meant to entice consumers to come to the store. Although marketers can do everything in their power to ensure that the consequence of the consumer's visit to their establishment is positive, first the consumer must initiate a visit. The ads and promotions make use of the operant conditioning principle *prompting*, essentially jump-starting the desired consumer behavior. Prompting is the rationale behind Burger King's policy of having servers ask consumers if they want to "King Size" their meal. Similarly Macy's cosmetics counterpersons always ask consumers if they need additional items.

> Prompt consumers' behavior.

THE DESTINATION IS REACHED A STEP AT A TIME

Prompting can initiate behavior. Then, once consumers are in the store, marketing efforts extend beyond initiating behavior to moving consumers closer to buying.

The warehouse store PriceCostco strives to make the customer's shopping experience something like going to a party and munching hors d'oeuvres. Customers are offered free samples of many food products, which are prepared in full view of shoppers by trained demonstrators. The aromas are tantalizing and inviting. As customers snack on the freshly prepared food, the demonstrators chat with customers, explaining the product's preparation and passing along other interesting tidbits of information. Long's Drug Store features in-store "manager's specials" that consumers learn of only when in the store shopping. Likewise, K-Mart is known for its "blue light specials": unscheduled, surprise sales on selected items in the store. The blue light specials run for a brief period of time (perhaps 15 minutes) and only shoppers who are in the store when the sale is announced know to take advantage of them. Signs in Mervyn's Department Store inform customers that they will receive a 10% discount on their purchases if they apply for a store credit card.

PriceCostco's free food samples, Long's "manager's specials," K-Mart's blue light specials, and Mervyn's discount are all efforts designed to move the consumer closer to making a purchase. If a consumer samples a product, he or she is more likely to buy it. If a consumer realizes that select store items are on sale, he or she will be more willing to consider a purchase. Getting a 10% discount on today's purchases by applying for a credit card may just make it worthwhile. Rewarding the consumer for behaviors that move them closer to the desired end behavior is exercising the operant conditioning principle called *shaping*.

> **Shape behavior with nudges and rewards.**

NEGATIVE REINFORCEMENT IS GOOD

Providing positive reinforcement or rewards for a behavior increase the probability that the behavior will occur again. Consumers will also increase the frequency of behaviors that *avoid* negative consequences or minimize or *eliminate* unpleasant situations.

Pepcid AC is a product for consumers whose desire to eat spicy foods is thwarted by the threat of heartburn and indigestion. Pepcid AC's advertising campaign advises these consumers to *avoid* heartburn and indigestion by taking the product before eating spicy foods. Pepcid AC is a negative reinforcement—consumers take Pepcid AC, eat spicy foods, and suffer no heartburn or indigestion. They next time they eat spicy foods, they will probably take Pepcid AC first.

Consumers who find that their pounding, throbbing headache is *eliminated* after taking an analgesic such as Tylenol will likely use the product again when they have a headache. Tylenol removed an aversive, unpleasant situation.

> **Preventing negative outcomes is reinforcing.**

CUE THE CONSUMER TO THE DESIRED BEHAVIOR

Marketers can design the environment to cue consumers to perform a desired behavior. For example, consumers will sit and rest at shopping malls—but only for a short time if the seating provided is composed of concrete slabs aesthetically decorated with ceramic tile. After a few minutes discomfort is elicited by compacted rear ends, and consumers are off again to do what they are supposed to do—shop.

The first person to arrive at a bench will likely sit toward one end. The next person will sit at the other end. The third person to arrive will sit between the first two but with plenty of room on either side. This process continues until the bench fills up. Designing bench seating to encourage social interaction can be accomplished by simply placing two cushions next to each other in the middle of the bench. This design will interrupt the normal bench-seating behavior of people. The first person to arrive will sit on a cushion because it is much more comfortable than the uncushioned area. The second person will likely opt to sit on the other cushion.

You form circles of seats if you want social interaction. You form a line of seats bolted to the ground if you want to discourage this behavior. Social interaction quickly becomes uncomfortable when you have to swivel your head and neck and twist your back to talk with the person sitting next to you. It's murder to have to stand or turn completely around to talk to someone seated behind you. Waiting rooms in public places such as train stations, bus stations, ferry stations, and airports normally have seating arranged in rows. The goal is to discourage social interaction because it discourages loitering.

Sit on the same side of the table with consumers to cue cooperative interaction. Sit on the opposite side of the table to cue competitive interaction.

> Environmental impact is not just a required ecological report. It's how you design the environment for consumer behavior.

VICARIOUS LEARNING, OBSERVATIONAL LEARNING, MODELING

Every year fairgoers look forward to the product demonstrations featured at county and state fairs. The demonstrators show consumers the wonders of their products: ever-sharp knives that cut steel as easily as they cut vegetables, two-headed mops that ease the chore of washing floors and walls, all-purpose cleaning fluids that eliminate the need for any other cleaners, and more. The demonstrators proclaim the benefits and advantages of their goods. The demonstrations hold the consumer's attention by being entertaining and fun. They sell a lot of products.

Martha Stewart, Emeril LaGasse, Martin Yan, Jeff Smith, Ming Tsai, and Graham Kerr each star in popular cooking shows on television. Loyal viewers learn how to prepare fabulous, mouth-watering dishes by observing the expert preparations step by step.

The success of Bob Villa's "This Old House" program rested in part on his friendly, avuncular dispensation of instruction, advice, and the do's and don'ts of home repair projects. Consumers learn by observing. They learn by watching others and then imitating the modeled behavior. This type of learning is called *vicarious learning,* or *observational learning.* Marketers should consider using vicarious learning for products or services that consumers find confusing or difficult to use. Live demonstrations, how-to clinics, or videos featuring demonstrations can be effective vehicles for vicarious learning. For example, Home Depot offers free seminars on a variety of home-improvement topics. Consumers attend the seminars, learn by observing the modeled behavior, and then buy the necessary materials—at Home Depot of course—to apply what they have learned.

The consumer sees and the consumer learns.

MEMORY

MAKE THE INFORMATION STICKY

When marketers present information to the consumer, they have two concerns. First, they want consumers to remember the information. Second, they want consumers to act on the information at the appropriate time.

The CEO featured in the television commercials for the Jack in the Box restaurant is a man impeccably dressed in a business suit with a giant, oversized jack-in-the-box head. This Jack in the Box CEO talks through a mouth that never moves, and speaks with an intercom-like voice full of emotion from a face that remains immobile. Consumers have seen the inanimate-faced CEO blush with embarrassment as he exchanges intimacies with his wife over the phone and shed tears of joy over the accomplishments of his young son, who also possesses a giant jack-in-the-box head. The consistent use of the jack-in-the-box head makes it impossible to watch these television commercials and not know that it is a Jack in the Box restaurant commercial. Consumers will never mistake a Jack in the Box commercial with one for McDonald's, Wendy's, Carl's Jr., Burger King or any other restaurant.

Focus a salient beam of light on the to-be-remembered product.

Chunking is the organizing and presenting of information so that it can be processed as a single unit. It is easier to remember a single unit than all of its components. The mnemonic "HOMES" makes it easier to remember the names of the five Great Lakes (i.e., Lake **H**uron, Lake **O**ntario, Lake **M**ichigan, Lake **E**rie, and Lake **S**uperior). It's easier to remember the twelve elements in the human body if we create a clever mnemonic such as "C HOPKINS CaFe Mg NaCl," in which Mg is "mighty good" and NaCl is salt: **C**arbon, **H**ydrogen, **O**xygen, **P**hosphorous, **P**otassium, **I**odine, **N**itrogen, **S**ulfur, **C**alcium, **I**ron, **M**agnesium, **S**odium, and **C**hloride. By the same token, it's easier for consumers to remember that the phone number of an optometrist is EYE-CARE instead of 393-2273.

Chunk many into one to facilitate memorization.

Raisins acquired personality when the California Raisin Board featured the California Dancing Raisins in a well-received advertising campaign. Consumers know that when you poke the Pillsbury Doughboy in the stomach he emits a warm-hearted giggle. Placing the California Dancing Raisins on packages of raisins reminds consumers of the advertisements. The Doughboy when featured on packages of Pillsbury products will remind consumers of the Doughboy's giggles.

Use cues to jog the consumer's memory.

Can you sing the jingle for each of the following products?

Campbell's Soup: "M'm, m'm good. That's what Campbell's Soups are—m'm, m'm good!"

L'eggs hosiery: "Our L'eggs fit your legs. They hold you. They hug you. They won't let you go."

Strive for tunes and jingles studded with clinging power.

Challenge the consumer to remember.

Some fishhooks not only have hooks on the end, but also hooks on the side. The extra hooks provide insurance that the "big one" will not get away. That's how memorable jingles and product songs work. They have barbs that give the jingles and songs clinging power.

Thirty years ago, McDonald's challenged consumers to remember all the ingredients in a Big Mac. To this day, many consumers who were exposed to this campaign can recite the ingredients: "Two all-beef patties, special sauce, lettuce, cheese, pickles, onions, on a sesame-seed bun."

5

ATTITUDE AND ATTITUDE CHANGE
I JUST FEEL LIKE BUYING IT

THE ABC'S OF ATTITUDE

Attitude is a state of mind important in explaining and predicting behavior. Consumers recognize the importance of attitude and its relationship to behavior. It dots everyday conversations: "Don't give me attitude!" "He has such a positive attitude toward life." Posters and tee shirts declare ATTITUDE = ALTITUDE , suggesting that consumers with a positive attitude can climb to unprecedented heights of accomplishments.

Affect, Behavior, and **Cognition** are the components of attitude. *Affect* is how the consumer feels, *behavior* refers to the consumer's actions or intentions, and *cognitions* are the consumer's beliefs and knowledge. The order of these ABC's is involved in the formation of attitude.

SITUATION ONE. A sweater is displayed on a realistic-looking mannequin. Customers who inadvertently bump into the mannequin find themselves apologizing. Then, feeling rather silly, they look around sheepishly to determine whether other customers witnessed their behavior. The display is very effective and makes the sweater look so good that many consumers buy it because they "just have to have it!" It is the combination of the mannequin's strategic placement and the soft lighting that makes the display successful.

SITUATION TWO. Golf pro shops encourage shoppers to take clubs to the driving range to try them out. They may even give customers a bucket of balls. Sporting goods stores allow customers to check out tennis racquets for a few days. This policy allows customers to get a good idea of what playing with a specific racquet feels like. Manufacturers of shampoos, cereals, detergents, and toothpaste distribute free samples with the home-delivered newspapers. Magazine advertisements offer readers a sampling of colognes, perfumes, and even lipstick.

SITUATION THREE. Washing machines and dryers are about as expensive as other household appliances like refrigerators, but they not nearly as visible.

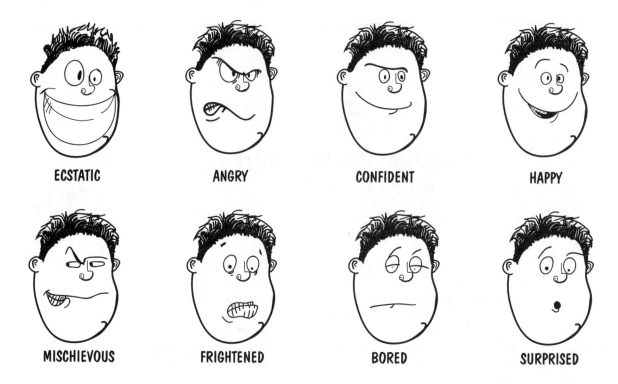

ECSTATIC   ANGRY   CONFIDENT   HAPPY

MISCHIEVOUS   FRIGHTENED   BORED   SURPRISED

Washing machines are often banished to the basement, laundry room, or garage. They are not interesting products and rarely become a topic of conversation. Although consumers frequently have warm, fuzzy feelings about their cars and may see their cars as extensions or personifications of themselves, consumers seldom—if ever—extend such feelings to their washing machines.

Washing machines are functional. Until water overflows from them or laundry comes out dirtier than when it went in, consumers do not give washing machines much thought. When washing machines need to be replaced, consumers seldom buy the first one they happen to see. It is more likely that they will visit several stores, talk to their friends, read *Consumer Reports,* and search the Internet.

ANALYSIS

Affect can initiate attitude formation.

In situation one, consumers fall in love with the sweater and buy it. They probably learn about the sweater (e.g., needs to be dry cleaned or goes well with other clothing) after they bring it home and wear it. The sequence of ABC's for this situation is affect, behavior, cognition.

Behavior can initiate attitude formation.

In situation two, consumers first try the product ("Why not, it's free!"). Then consumers decide whether or not they like the product. Finally, they form an opinion about the product ("This is great! I like it."). The sequence in this situation is behavior, affect, cognition.

Situation three is a high-involvement situation. The decision is important to consumers. The purchase of a washing machine involves a large sum of money, and the appliance will be with them for many years. Consumers gather information, consider the alternatives, and choose a model. In this situation, the sequence of ABCs is cognition, affect, behavior.

> Cognition can initiate attitude formation.

Not All Product Attributes Are Equal in the Eyes of the Consumers

If a marketer boasts that a brand is cheaper and more durable than the competition's, this does not make the brand desirable to consumers if consumers want style and color selection—not lower price and greater durability. It really doesn't matter if the marketer's product is better than the competitor's on product characteristics that are unimportant to consumers. What matters to consumers is how this brand stacks up against the competition on product characteristics they feel are important. Begin by finding out which product attributes are important to consumers.

> Pay attention to the important stuff.

Customer Satisfaction

In golf, tennis, and other sports, follow-through is important to success. You don't swing a golf club half way or stop the tennis racquet after it makes contact with the ball. You have to follow through. There is a balance, beauty, and symmetry that comes with the follow-through. The zing of a tennis serve and the thwack of a golf club contacting the ball is incomplete without follow-through. Don't just sell customers the product. Follow through. Clerks at some clothing stores stuff the articles of clothing in the bag. Clerks at other stores fold and bag the clothes with care and expertise.

> Follow-through really matters.

In his book *Selling the Invisible,* Harry Beckwith tells the story of taking a pair of his favorite shoes to a cobbler to be repaired. When Harry goes back to pick up his shoes, he finds a note of apology informing him that his shoes have been worn beyond repair. Inside each shoe, wrapped in tissue paper, is a cookie.[1]

The marketing function does not end with the sale. Follow-up is necessary in high-involvement situations in which cognitive dissonance may arise, causing consumers to doubt the wisdom of their choices. Marketing strategy should include one or more contacts following the sale to answer consumers' questions and reassure them of the wisdom of their choice.

> Assure the consumer of the wisdom of his or her choice.

Tiger Woods's performance at the 1997 Masters so unquestionably outdistanced his nearest competitor's that commentators suggested the Augusta course be redesigned to make it more challenging for Woods. Marketers, too, must recognize that their competitors will keep raising the bar of consumer expectations. In the 1980s, Japanese car manufacturers raised the standards of quality and excellence. Consumers expected all cars, not just Japanese cars, to meet these superior standards. When American-manufactured cars failed to meet these expectations, consumers' lack of satisfaction was noted by lowered sales.

Consumer satisfaction occurs only when expectations are confirmed or surpassed. At a minimum, marketers must meet the established standards that customers have come to expect. Marketers must be on guard and vigilant in recognizing the ever-rising bar of consumer expectations or must be among the leaders who raise it. Calloway established a new standard in golf clubs. Prince established the importance of tennis racquet head size.

ENGLISH 1A IN ADVERTISING

The goal of advertisements is not only to inform but also to persuade. Information can be presented in a literal fashion or in a rhetorical manner. Advertisements that use rhetorical devices put a twist on the familiar by incorporating clever, artful deviations that result in greater consumer recall and persuasiveness.

CONCENTRATED STAIN MAKER.   CONCENTRATED STAIN REMOVER.

Remove tough stains - from grass to grease - with Shout® Concentrated Gel. The power of a gel. The penetration of a brush. Really tough stains have just met their match.

Shout Concentrated Gel. Want a tough stain out? Shout it out!®

Little boys are known to be rough on their clothes. You don't have to ask little boys what they had for lunch—just look at their clothes and you know that they had spaghetti and chocolate ice cream. The grass stains and dirt that cover their clothes let you know that they have been busy playing in dirt, exploring in bushes, and rolling around on grass. Identifying a boy as a "concentrated stain maker" is humorous.

CURE BALDNESS

Kretschmer Wheat Germ.
It can't promise to grow hair on your head. But it can top your favorite ice cream with natural vitamins, minerals and fiber—plus a delicious, crunchy taste.

That's because Kretschmer is the heart of the wheat—the storehouse of concentrated nutrition.

So add Honey Crunch Kretschmer to your ice cream—or frozen yogurt—and see what its delicious crunch and great nutrition can do for you!

**Kretschmer.
It's the Heart of the Wheat.**

The headline "Cure Baldness" leads the reader to expect a product to replace hair loss. Curing "bald" ice cream with wheat germ topping is an unexpected, clever twist and leaves the reader with a smile.[2]

FEAR APPEALS

Fear motivates people to act. Consumers can be scared into protecting their homes, cars, and even themselves with alarms. Consumers can be convinced to buy health insurance, car insurance, homeowners' insurance, flood insurance, and earthquake insurance because they fear unexpected events. Although people will act out of fear, they don't like to feel afraid. Using fear appeals means balancing these two opposing forces. Fear appeals must be sufficiently scary to move people into action, but not so scary that they can't even consider it.

The advertisement features a close-up of what looks like splats of blood on the floor. The camera records the person as he slowly follows the trail of blood. Finally, he finds the source of the blood—a person eating a Carl's Jr. hamburger. Viewers then realize that the splats are catsup that dripped out as the peripatetic consumer ate his hamburger. Consumer dislike of this commercial was sufficiently vociferous to squelch the campaign. Fear appeals are not appropriate for all products. Fear appeals work for those products designed to meet what Abraham Maslow (see p. 36) defined as the consumer's safety and security needs—e.g., insurance, health care, and retirement funds.

> Scare people to action.

HUMOR APPEALS

People like to laugh and have a good time. Humor is good for you. The magazine *Reader's Digest* has a column titled "Laughter, the Best Medicine." The Sunday paper is special because the comics are printed in color. Dilbert is the protagonist of best-selling books, specializing in humorous interpretations of cubicle office workers. If you can see humor in a situation, it doesn't seem so bad.

The humor should match the product and the situation. Otherwise, consumers may get the joke but forget the advertised product. This is known as the "vampire effect," when the humor sucks attention away from the advertised product.

The use of humor requires care and attention to not unintentionally offend. What is humorous to some may be offensive to others. Elderly consumers did not find the Wendy's advertisements depicting a little old lady driving recklessly from fast food restaurant to fast food restaurant asking "Where's the beef?" particularly funny.[3]

> Leave 'em laughing and feeling good about your product.

THE GOOD AND THE BAD

Not everything is perfect for everyone. Sometimes you may be more convincing by admitting that along with your strengths, you have weaknesses. It makes you more believable.

Marketers for L'Oréal recognize the product's shortcoming. It's expensive. But the shortcoming viewed from the vantage point of the consumer's self-worth is transformed into something positive. L'Oréal invites consumers to pamper themselves with a product that is more expensive than competing products because they—the consumers—are worth it.

"We're number two, but we try harder" is an Avis Rent-A-Car advertising campaign that admits a shortcoming to emphasize a strength (i.e., *being number two makes us try harder to serve customers*—or *being number two in sales makes us number one in service*).

> You're more believable if you're not perfect.

PRINCIPLES OF SALESMANSHIP

RECIPROCITY

The social norm of reciprocity forms the basis of a number of successful selling techniques.

DOOR-IN-THE-FACE

Ask for a ridiculously large favor and expect rejection. Then ask for a smaller favor and expect compliance. This is the "door-in-the-face" technique. The request for a ridiculously large favor will get the door slammed in the requester's face, but will lead to a higher probability of compliance for the smaller favor, which was the intention to begin with. If you reduce your request, the consumer reciprocates by agreeing.

In one experiment, a person approached students on their way to class and asked them if they would volunteer to take juveniles to the zoo for two hours. Seventeen percent agreed. In a second experiment, a person approached students and asked them if they would volunteer to work at a juvenile detention center for two years. Of course they all refused. The students were then asked to take a group of juveniles to the zoo for two hours. Fifty percent agreed.[4]

EVEN A PENNY

Ask for a donation and end with the statement "even a penny [dollar] will help." People are more willing to help when the request legitimizes a paltry amount; the average amount given using this appeal is equivalent to the amount given by those contributions received through a direct appeal.[5]

THAT'S NOT ALL

Infomercials offer a product for a price, throw in a host of free accessories, and then lower the price if consumers order within the next ten minutes. The marketer increases the value of the offer, and consumers reciprocate by complying.[6]

CONSISTENCY

People like consistency, harmony and balance in their lives. They like to see the world this way, and they will behave in a consistent manner as the following selling techniques illustrate.

FOOT-IN-THE-DOOR

Make a small request: ask a small favor for which there is a high probability of compliance. Get a foot in the door. Then make the large request. Compliance is higher with the foot-in-the-door technique than by directly asking for the larger request. People comply with the small request and, to remain consistent, comply with the larger request.

In a door-to-door campaign, consumers were asked a small favor: post a small "Be a Safe Driver" sign. When agreement was obtained, they were then asked to post a large sign on their front lawns and 76% complied. A direct request to post the large sign resulted in 17% compliance.[7]

LOWBALL

Start with a ridiculously low price to lure customers. Hook the customer by getting them to agree to buy the ridiculously low-priced product. Then explain why the price has to be increased to a higher, more realistic level (e.g., error in the calculations). Consumers committed to buy at the low price will commit to the higher price to remain consistent.

Students on their way to class were asked if they would take part in an experiment. Fifty-six percent agreed to participate. When then told that the experiment was scheduled for 7:00 A.M. on a Saturday, 53% actually showed up. In contrast, only 31% of students agreed to participate when asked directly to participate in an experiment scheduled for 7:00 A.M. on a Saturday, and only 24% actually showed up.[8]

6

PERSONALITY AND SELF-CONCEPT
BUY IT. IT LOOKS JUST LIKE YOU.

MARKETING ACCORDING TO FREUD

In Freudian personality theory, symbols are important vehicles to communicate with the subconscious, a component of personality.

Functionally the purpose of these bottles is to store perfume and cologne; symbolically, however, they may communicate much more.

The shapes of the perfume bottles are phallic. The intent is to communicate this at the subconscious level. At the conscious level, consumers would most likely be offended if antiperspirant or perfume was sold in containers that were more realistic models of the male sexual organ.

In Freudian theory, sex is one of the main motivators of human behavior. Often the sexual motivations for behavior are rooted in the subconscious; consequently the consumers themselves are not aware of them.

Marketers embraced the tenets of Freudian theory after World War II when evangelists such as Ernest Ditcher successfully spread its application to marketing. Its influence on marketing is best illustrated by comparing the use of sex in advertising before and after the insertion of Freudian theory into marketing.

Sex sells.

Is there something wrong with the ad for Banner House? It may not be obvious to consumers upon first glance, but a closer inspection reveals the incongruity. The woman's leg is in an impossible position.

SUBLIMINAL SEDUCTION

ARE YOU BEING SEXUALLY AROUSED BY THIS PICTURE?

Look at the ice cubes in the glass. Has something been airbrushed in the ice cubes? Is there really an "overly endowed" boy standing on the lemon wedge?

Subliminal sex sells.

Sex in Pre-Freudian advertising can be described as innocent or romantic. In Post-Freudian advertising, phallic symbolism (e.g., guns) makes its appearance, sex is made provocative by what is *not* shown, and a general trend toward a more explicit display of sex is evident.

In this advertisement for Bushmills Premium Irish Whiskey, is the positioning of the bottles and the presentation of the whiskey pouring into the glass designed to suggest sexual activities?

WHEN A WHISPER IS MORE EFFECTIVE THAN A SCREAM

Subliminal perception occurs below conscious awareness. Do the pictures below really contain hidden, *subliminal* elements? Do you see sexual elements in the pictures?

In Freudian theory, Thanatos, or the death wish, is the other primary motivator of human behavior. Do you see ghoulish, death mask–like faces in the pictures below?

There are skulls and ghoulish faces in the ice cubes. Does this mean that consumers are drinking themselves to death?

It doesn't matter whether marketers believe in Freudian theory. Elements of Freudian theory have become a permanent part of everyday life.

THE ID, THE EGO, AND THE SUPEREGO

Freudian theory posits three components of personality: id, ego, and superego. Conflict is inevitable in Freudian theory. For the id, pleasure, fun, and instant gratification are the raisons d'être. For the superego, moralistic imperatives and

Nuance always says Yes. But you can always say No.

This ad for Nuance perfume appeals to the id while it placates the superego. The consumer follows the moralistic imperatives of the superego and says no. The perfume says yes and fulfills the desires of the id.

admonitions are the rules by which life must be lived. The fun-filled, carefree, and sinful desires of the id are in direct conflict with the perfectionist, moralistic demands of the superego. The ego attempts to balance the demands of the id and superego within the limits and confines of the physical world.

Market to the id, ego, and superego.

Introducing Quorum. A cologne for the other man lurking inside you.

Eau de toilette, spray cologne, after shave.

At Emporium-Capwell

The man featured in the ad for the cologne is well groomed, professionally dressed, and exudes success. He is socialized and fulfills the demands of the superego. Lurking beneath the well-polished surface is the id.

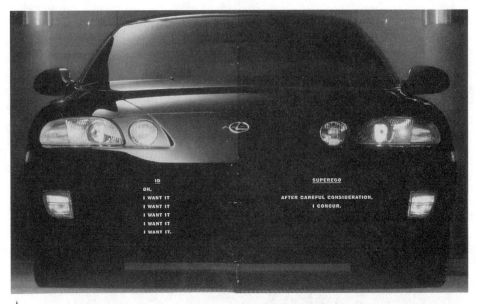

The car featured in this ad meets the demands of both the id and superego.

JUNG AND ARCHETYPES

The psychologist Carl Jung believed in the inheritance of the cumulative experiences of past generations. This inheritance is the basis of archetypes, universally shared ideas and behavioral patterns.

Perhaps one explanation for these long-lived, memorable brand images is their archetypical embodiment. Betty Crocker and Aunt Jemima, for example, are nurturing, maternal archetypes. Virginia Slims is the archetype of the sexy superwoman, exuding confidence and independence.

The Quaker Oats Man is a paternal archetype, conveying old-fashioned goodness. Other mythical great-father archetypes are the Maytag repairman, who is dependable, protective, and caring; Mr. Goodwrench, who is protective, trustworthy, reassuring, and knowledgeable; and Mr. Clean, the wizard archetype who magically transforms dirtiness to cleanliness.

Hidden Valley represents an archetypical place: a paradise that is green, lush, peaceful, comforting, and safe.

CONSUMER SELF-CONCEPT

BEAUTY IS IN VOGUE . . . AND IN *Glamour*, AND *GQ*

Consumers evaluate their appearance based upon current standards of beauty. These standards change over time, and what is now considered beautiful may have been undesirable just a short time ago.

The characteristics of desirable lips have changed over time. Thin lips have given way to fuller lips. Eyebrows have thinned, thickened, and thinned again.

BEAUTY CHANGES OVER TIME

Current benchmark of beauty: Cindy Crawford.

Jean Shrimpton, 1970s.

Twiggy, 1960s.

Past benchmark of beauty.

THE BIOLOGY OF BEAUTY[1,2,3,4,5]

According to beauty scientists, the fact that Denzel Washington and Leonardo DiCaprio turn heads and people find supermodels Cindy Crawford and Naomi Campbell attractive may have a biologic basis.

Symmetrical faces indicate a good skeletal structure, strong immune system, and good mental health (less manic depression, anxiety, and schizophrenia.)

As different as they look, Venus de Milo, Marilyn Monroe, Kate Moss, Twiggy, and Alek Wek all have waist-to-hip ratios between 0.6 and 0.7. Although there may be a few hundred pounds difference between Ruben's Renaissance beauty and the pencil-thin, waif-like Kate Moss of the 1990s, proportionality of the waist-to-hip ratio appears to be the beauty constant.

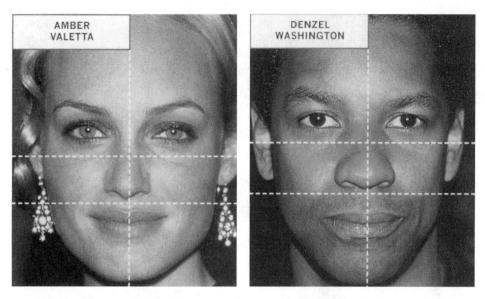

People find symmetrical faces attractive: eyes that are equal distance from the nose and ears set evenly from the chin.

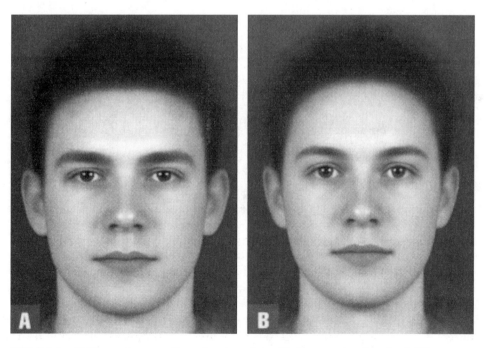

Which is best? Women's perception of men varies with the menstrual cycle. **A.** More-masculine faces look best near ovulation. **B.** Otherwise, more-feminine faces rule.

Michelangelo's David, Tyrone Power, and the current male supermodels have the ideal male waist-to-hip ratio of 0.9. Biologically, a washboard stomach and trim waistline indicate physical fitness and good health.

An interesting recent finding is women's preference for men with more masculine-looking faces during fertile times in their menstrual cycles while preferring feminine-looking faces for long-term relationships. One explanation is that men with more-feminine features may be more sensitive and nurturing, traits that would make them good fathers. This could explain the popularity of Leonardo DiCaprio, Elvis Presley, and Matt Damon.

| LEONARDO DICAPRIO | ELVIS PRESLEY | MATT DAMON |

Cultural definitions of beauty may change over time, but recent findings suggest that perhaps symmetry and proportionality are biological constants.

CONSUMERS HAVE MULTIPLE SELVES

Consumers have multiple selves, but we are not talking about multiple personalities or psychological disorders. Rather, people are like multi-faceted diamonds with many different dimensions to them.

CONSUMER IMAGE = BRAND IMAGE

Under the watch of CEO Louis Gerstner, IBM's brand turnaround is the biggest marketing achievement of the 1990s. Six years ago, IBM was perceived as big, stuffy, arrogant and a laggard in changing technology. Today IBM is synonymous with e-business and is perceived as a leader in Internet commerce. IBM changed its brand personality, an extraordinarily difficult task. What is even more extraordinary is that IBM did this without any real change in its lines of products and services.

Brand image is the company's most sacred asset. It is the company's identity.

How did IBM do this? In 1994, a decentralized IBM that spoke through seventy different advertising agencies was consolidated. The Ogilvy & Mather advertising agency became IBM's singular voice. In 1995, Ogilvy & Mather launched the "Solutions for a small planet" campaign featuring vignettes illustrating how IBM

Brands have established personalities, and consumers buy the products for their personalities as much as for the functional performance of the products.

technology helps people improve their lives. In 1997, IBM and Ogilvy & Mather coined the term "e-business" and trademarked the red "e" logo (see below), which was featured in clever commercials.[6]

SMALL GROUPS AND WORD-OF-MOUTH COMMUNICATION

HMMM ... I WONDER WHAT MY FRIENDS WOULD THINK.

REFERENCE GROUPS ARE THE CONSUMER'S REFERENCE POINTS

Reference groups are institutions, individuals, or groups—imagined or real—who serve as vital reference points that help consumers define their reality. Consumers want to be like the people they admire, revere, and respect. They will emulate them, aspire to be like them, and identify with them. Consumers will buy what they buy.

"I AM TIGER WOODS." "I WANT TO BE LIKE MIKE."

Nike understands the concept of reference groups. Tiger Woods and Michael Jordan are reference groups to millions of consumers. His Airness Michael Jordan helped establish Nike as a dominant brand of the 1980s. Millions of consumers wanted to be like Mike. So, like Mike, they ate Ball Park hot dogs, donned Hanes underwear, drank Gatorade, started their morning with a bowl of Wheaties cereal, and, of course, wore Nike tennis shoes.

Tiger Woods is a hero to many young golfers. Their affinity for Tiger Woods is so strong that many declare, "I am Tiger Woods."

The spokesperson must match the product in the consumer's mind. John Houseman, well known for his role as the staid, conservative, and serious Professor Kingsfield of the television series *Paper Chase*, was selected as a spokesperson for McDonald's. Wrong choice. John Houseman/Professor Kingsfield and McDonald's just don't go together. It is quite inconceivable that Professor Kingsfield would ever eat at McDonald's.

Lock and key. They have to match.

DEAD CELEBS

Spokespersons, like Michael Jordan and Tiger Woods, can add value to the product's brand image, increase consumer awareness and recall, and build market share. But spokespersons are real people. And real people can, and do, make mistakes. Unfortunately, a celebrity's faux pas is magnified and sometimes even vilified. Ideal Toys' launch of an Evel Knievel action figure was quashed when the daredevil took a baseball bat to a news reporter he didn't fancy. Burt Reynolds was a spokesperson for the Florida Orange Board until his nasty, acrimonious, bitter, name-calling, public divorce from Loni Anderson forced his dismissal. Michael Jackson's child-molestation charges made Pepsi reconsider, and eventually stop, using him to promote their products. (Besides, Michael Jackson does not drink Pepsi.) Pepsi also dropped Mike Tyson as a spokesperson when media reports claimed he used his boxing skills on his wife, Robin Givens.

Celebrity spokespersons' missteps can negatively affect the products that they are endorsing. One way around this is to use dead celebrities. Dead celebrities have solid, well-established public personas and are guaranteed not to embarrass or soil the product they are championing. Dead celebrities are very well behaved.

Dead celebrities have solid, well-established public personas.

Not in the United States, but in Japan

To maintain their public persona, movie stars such as Jodi Foster, Harrison Ford, Steven Seagal, and Brad Pitt opt not to serve as spokespersons for products in the United States but gladly do so in Japan, where the use of American celebrities adds cachet to the advertisement product.

Real People

Timex, the watch that "Takes a Licking and Keeps on Ticking," featured real people who "took a licking and kept on ticking" in its advertisements. Read about these real people.

> "Louisa Murray was eating a sandwich when a bowling ball fell off a ledge three stories above and hit her in the head. Doctors gave her a one in a million chance, but she fought back and last spring graduated from college. The ball did leave a 'little dent' in her head." (In the ad, Louisa is shown wearing a Timex women's fashion watch.)

> "Keith Moody was afraid he lost his baby, Tanner, after a tornado destroyed his home, until he heard faint crying from above. He found Tanner, relatively unhurt, hanging upside down in a tree eight feet from the ground. His sleeper had caught on a limb." (The ad describes Tanner as snagging onto a water-resistant Timex Gizmoz watch for kids.)

> "John Scott was in a 480-foot mine elevator in England when safety engineers began testing its emergency braking system. The engineers repeatedly raised the elevator to the surface and sent it into a free-fall before realizing John and a fellow miner were inside. They survived the two-hour ordeal with some very sore backs." (John is shown wearing the Timex B-29 chronograph watch.)

> "Kathy Nelson was spun at high speed, virtually upside down, for nearly half an hour on a carnival ride when it got stuck in "high gear." The ride—a spinning disk that rises until it's perpendicular to the ground—generates so much velocity that riders are held in by centrifugal force. It usually lasts four minutes." (Kathy is shown wearing a basic Timex watch.)

> "Lorraine Lengkeek was hiking down a trail in Glacier National Park, singing "How Great Thou Art," when a grizzly bear appeared and attacked her husband Deane. She fought off the bear by whacking it on the nose with her binoculars and then used her bra as a tourniquet to stop Dean's bleeding." (In the ad, Lorraine is wearing a Timex Camper watch with the IndiGlo night light.)

The Most Believable Advertisements are Not Advertisements

In the movie *GoldenEye*, the unflappable British secret service agent James Bond, accompanied by the ever-present beautiful woman, roars down the country road in a state-of-the-art BMW. In *Back to the Future*, Marty McFly, played by Michael J. Fox, orders a Pepsi Free. The old folks eat Quaker Oats in *Cocoon*. In *Happy Gilmore*, Adam Sandler's hockey-player-turned-golf-pro character is shown teeing off a Subway sandwich into a customer's open mouth—talk about a hole in one. In *Austin Powers: The Spy Who Shagged Me,* Heineken beer is featured. Get the picture? These are advertisements that are not advertisements.

These products don't appear by accident in these movies. They were intentionally put there by product placers who pay for products to be shown in movies. These advertisements are seamlessly interfaced with the movie, so consumers do not interpret them as advertisements. They are much more believable and effective.

'Tis Better to Give, For Then You Shall Receive

Tommy Hilfiger took a tip from sporting goods manufacturers like Nike and Reebok and gave his clothes to hip-hop performers like The Fugees. When The Fugees wear Tommy Hilfiger clothes, Tommy Hilfiger clothes become cool and sales become very hot.

When 3M first advertised Post-It Notes, it didn't work. Then 3M gave Post-It Notes to secretaries. Secretaries put them on work they sent to their bosses, on routing slips, and on interoffice paperwork. Post-It Notes began showing up on telephones as reminders to make a call. Soon Post-It Notes was known around the world.

When Gillette developed erasable-ink EraserMate pens, it gave away sixty thousand of them to schoolteachers, bankers, and senators. When other people saw them use these erasable ink pens, they wanted an EraserMate, too.

When Chrysler introduced its LH series of cars—the Dodge Intrepid, Chrysler Concord, and Eagle Vision—dealers in several states offered LH models to over six thousand influential community leaders and business executives for a weekend's use. A follow-up survey showed that the cars received a total of thirty-two thousand exposures in three months, including secondary drivers and passengers. More than 98% of those responding said they would recommend the car to a friend, and 90% said their opinion of Chrysler had improved.[1]

New York City's Kirshenbaum & Bond Advertising devised a clever way to use word of mouth communication to open up new markets for its client, Hennessy Cognac. The agency created a "brandy martini" (a shot of chilled brandy and a squeeze of lime). It hired actors to go into bars in major markets and stage loud arguments. The amicable resolution included one of the actors loudly yelling to the bartender, "Hennessy martinis all around."[1]

Blab, Blab, Blab. Yak, Yak, Yak.

Mountain Dew is a leading soft drink of Generation Y (teens) thanks in large part to word-of-mouth communication among Gen Y members that Mountain Dew is loaded with more caffeine than Coca-Cola.

In the mid-1990s, sneakers with the 1960s "retro" look, like the Adidas trademark stripes and Puma "Clydes" (named after the former New York Knicks star Walt "Clyde" Frazier), became a must-have item among Generation X'ers. The retro look was a red-hot fad that eventually faded, but it did have a solid impact on the athletic shoe market. The interesting thing about this fad is that it was powered by word-of-mouth communication. Except for Converse, who ran small ads in Gen X magazines like *Thrasher* and *Dirt*, there was zero advertising.[2]

The "Honda Syndrome" has infected a lot of 18- to 30-year-olds in southern California and is spreading across the South to the East Coast. It has earned the University of California at Irvine the nickname "University of Civics and Integras." The Civic coupes and hatchbacks are coveted for their low suspension, affordability, easy-to-modify engine, and sporty looks. The availability of performance-enhancing parts and accessories allows consumers to have fun creatively customizing, modifying, and souping up their cars: "a set of bigger, fancier wheel rims, smaller, thinner tires, a shiny exhaust system; body skirts; air dams mounted on the front end; and rear 'wings.'" Honda Motor Co. executives had nothing to do with the surge in Honda popularity and do not understand it, but they are not complaining. The Honda Syndrome has boosted the retail price of a used 1996 Civic DX coup to $12,700, $420 more than the original showroom price. In 1997, a year when sales of small cars declined, U.S. sales of Civics jumped 9 percent to 315,546.[3]

Opinion leaders offer suggestions and advice that consumers judge to be more believable than the same message delivered by marketer-dominated forms of communication such as television commercials, direct mailings, and print advertisements. Identify opinion leaders and give them or loan them the product. It is well worth it because they, in turn, will broadcast your product to other consumers. Opinion leaders will multiply the value of your gift to them.

To truly understand the social power of opinion leaders, consider the following example suggested by Malcolm Gladwell in his book, *The Tipping Point*. If you take a piece of paper and fold it in half, then fold it in half again, then fold that in half again, and so on, how thick do you think it would be when you have refolded it fifty times? As thick as the Manhattan telephone directory? As tall as a refrigerator? Not many people would imagine that the height would approximate the distance to the sun! This is what the power of opinion leaders is like. Opinion leaders are people with the ability to use word-of-mouth communication to spread the word geometrically.[4]

> Opinion leaders are your best evangelists.

SAY IT AIN'T SO

What do Pop Rocks candy, Bubble Yum bubble gum, Corona beer, the Procter & Gamble logo, McDonald's hamburgers, Snapple drinks, and Tropical Fantasy soft drink all have in common? They have all been the victims of negative word-of-mouth communication. Pop Rocks is a novelty candy made with encapsulated carbon dioxide that causes the candy chunks to pop with crackling sounds when eaten. Rumors circulated in schoolyards that Pop Rocks exploded in your stomach, cut holes in your throat and caused the death of little Mikey (of Life Cereal fame), whose stomach allegedly exploded upon drinking a Coke shortly after eating a packet of Pop Rocks. Bubble Yum bubble gum, the most exciting innovation in gum since sugarless, stays soft chew after chew and allows consumers to blow gigantic bubbles. However, it was plagued with rumors that it contained spider eggs and gave consumers brain cancer. There was buzz that Corona beer was tainted with cow urine. Tropical Fantasy soft drink sales declined after negative word-of-mouth publicity claimed that it caused sterilization in black men. Rumors circulated that the K on the Snapple label stood for Ku Klux Klan, when in reality the K stood for kosher. Far from being just silly and fun, rumors can hurt sales. Would you eat at McDonald's if you heard that its hamburgers were made with worms or horse meat? Would you buy Procter & Gamble products if your friends told you that the company's success was due to devil worship, as evidenced by its man-in-the-moon logo? Supposedly the stars spell out 6-6-6—symbols used in satanic worship.

In 1993 Pepsi was accused of being involved in product tampering. A couple in Tacoma, Washington, found a used syringe in a can of Diet Pepsi. They contacted their lawyer, who notified the press and local health officials who, in turn, alerted the police. Within days, fifty similar complaints in 23 states were recorded. It soon became clear that many (perhaps all) of the reported cases were hoaxes committed by copycats who were motivated by a need for attention, or by scam artists looking for personal-injury compensation. The frenzy around the Pepsi product-tampering scare fizzled, but not before Pepsi Cola took out full-page ads in newspapers around the country declaring the whole episode to be a hoax.[5]

Stifle the rumors. In such situations, marketing wisdom tells us to meet the rumors head on. Use advertisements, press releases, or have company executives appear on talk shows to say it ain't so.

REFERENCE GROUPS BENCHMARK CONSUMERS

Question: Are you beautiful, smart, successful, or athletic? Answer: It depends on the reference groups with whom you compare yourself.

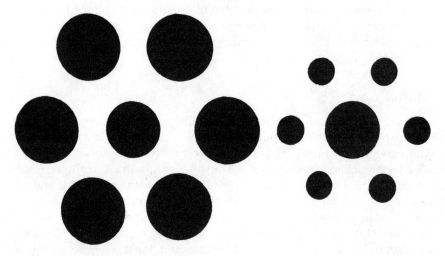

Which center circle is larger?

The size of the center circle is identical in each picture. Surrounded by larger circles, the center circle appears smaller. Surrounded by smaller circles, the center circle appears larger.

How consumers measure up depends on their choice of rulers, or reference groups. Arguably, consumers do have the freedom to choose their rulers, but then again it may be hard not to compare themselves with flawless, too-beautiful, too-successful, too-good-to-be-true, cool spokespersons who appear in magazine ads, loom from billboards, and find their way from television commercials into the consumer's living room.

Marketers rule with the consumers' choice of rulers.

8

SUBCULTURES
BIRDS OF A FEATHER FLOCK TOGETHER

SOCIAL CLASSES

When you drive through different neighborhoods, you soon notice a similarity. In some neighborhoods, domestic cars are popular while other neighborhoods are populated with imports. In some neighborhoods you seem to find golf bags and golf clubs in every garage; in other neighborhoods golf clubs do not occupy a single garage. If we were to analyze the garbage produced by each household, it should not surprise us to learn that consumers who live in the same neighborhood read the same magazines, eat the same brands of foods, and use the same brands of toiletries.

These similarities within neighborhoods are the basis of **geodemographic clustering**. Geodemographic clustering combines demographic and socioeconomic data obtained from the U.S. census with consumer behavior data obtained from panel and survey studies. The result is an identification and description of the consumer behavior of residents from geographically defined neighborhoods.

> Your zip code reveals more than your address.

CHICKENS AND PEOPLE HAVE PECKING ORDERS

In the barnyard a pecking order exists. Some chickens are higher up in the hierarchy and have greater access to food and mates. People, like chickens, also have a pecking order. Social class is universal. Although every society has a social stratification system, the size and number of social classes differs from country to country, as illustrated on p. 78. Japan and Scandinavia, for example, both have a large middle class, while Latin America and India have larger lower classes. The United States, like Japan and Scandinavia, has a large number of people in the middle classes; however, unlike Japan and Scandinavia, the United States also has substantial numbers of people in the upper and lower classes.

> Social class is a universal with variations in size and number.

U.S. SOCIAL CLASSES

Consumers in different social classes are distinguished by different lifestyles, values, financial resources, and consumer behavior.

The "upper crust" consists of individuals with well-established family names (such as Kennedy, Vanderbilt, Rockefeller, DuPont, Getty, and Ford) and inherited wealth, or "old money." Bill Ford, Jr., has been crowned the CEO of Ford Motor Co., the company that his great-grandfather Henry Ford founded.

Unlike the other social classes in the United States, the upper crust is a closed society where membership is conferred by birth. Although marriage from a lower social class into the upper crust is possible, acceptance as an equal is not always forthcoming.

People in the "nouveau riche" social class have newly earned money. The distinction between the upper crust and the nouveau riche is not the amount of

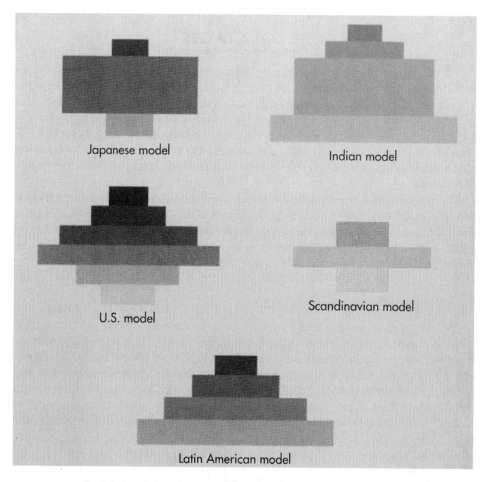

Social class is a universal with variations in size and number.

BusinessWeek

A PUBLICATION OF THE McGRAW-HILL COMPANIES

SEPTEMBER 28, 1998 / $3.95

Global Crisis
The G-7 to the rescue?

The Yankees
Inside baseball's richest team

Craig McCaw
He's back—with a bold new vision

Citicorp & Travelers
Does the deal still make sense?

CHAIRMAN FORD
His Roots, His Role, His Priorities
PAGE 96

BILL FORD, HENRY'S GREAT-GRANDSON

Old money.

money, but the age of the money. Like fine wine, upper crust money must be aged. The nouveau riche may have more financial resources than those in the upper crust, but their money is newly acquired—not inherited—and they do not have a well-established family name.

New money.

Consumer behavior differs among the social classes. The schism between the "haves" and "have nots" is the widest it has been since the 1930s, when the U.S. government began keeping records. Consumers employed in the new, information-and-technology–driven sector belong to the haves, while consumers employed in the industrial sector belong to the have-nots. The have-not sector produces tangible goods and services (e.g., health-care workers, educators, and restaurant workers).

Although differences in consumer behavior exist among the social classes, commonalities also exist. High brow, upper class consumption is different from low brow, lower class consumption. But for some things, "no brow" is more aptly descriptive.

> *High Brow:* Classical music, opera, ballet, rare wines, expensive art collections, exclusive country clubs, pedigree, private schools.
>
> *Low Brow:* Velvet paintings, plastic flowers, wrestling, cheap wines, plastic pink flamingos, bowling.
>
> *No Brow:* MTV, Wal-Mart, Target, McDonald's.

It's not quite fair: the haves and the have nots.

High brow, low brow, and maybe no brow.

SOCIAL CLASS IS MORE THAN JUST HOW MUCH MONEY YOU HAVE

In the best-selling book *The Millionaire Next Door,* authors Thomas Stanley and William Danko reveal the surprisingly modest lifestyle of the millionaire next door. The millionaire next door became wealthy because he or she is adept at financial offensive strategy (earning money) and even more adept at financial defensive strategy (how to spend money to get the best value, how to invest money to earn the best return). Millionaires are entrepreneurs in dull to normal businesses who earn good incomes (median income $131,000) and are fastidious investors. They choose to live comfortably, but below their means. They buy inexpensive off-the-rack suits, previously owned (used) cars, and may even clip coupons for grocery items. In general they are tightwads, but not when it comes to education. Millionaires believe education is important for themselves as well as their children and grandchildren, and they will spend heavily for their family's education expenses.[1]

Amy Dacyczyn and her husband, Jim, had a combined annual income of $30,000. In seven years they paid off their debts, bought two new cars, made a $49,000 down payment on a new house, and bought new home appliances. Oh, by the way, they also have six children. Amy Dacyczyn authored *The Tightwad Gazette* to explain how they accomplished this seemingly impossible feat. Now that Dacyczyn earns a six-figure income, she and her husband still choose to live the same lifestyle—after all, they want to put six children through college.[2,3]

Social class is how consumers choose to spend their money.

WHEN TEN DOLLARS IS ONE DOLLAR

It costs more to live in some parts of the United States than others. You give pause, however, when you learn that the average price of a home is $410,000 (more than twice the national average); the rent for an everyday, run-of-the-mill, one-bedroom apartment starts at $1,100; and people earning $37,000 are eligible for low-income housing programs. This is the cost of living in Silicon Valley, where an estimated 64 new "cybermillionaires" are made each day, and the average income is $82,600. Teachers, policemen, firemen, as well as the service providers in restaurants, hotels, and retail outlets are finding the cost of living unaffordable, and their exodus is threatening the social-service infrastructure as well as the quality of

The cost of living
redefines the
meaning of
income.

talent that high-tech business is able to recruit.[4] With its surplus of millionaires, Santa Clara County may be the heart of Silicon Valley; however, with 68,000 more single men than women, it apparently is also a lonely heart.[5]

IT'S TOO GOOD TO BE TRUE[6]

Consumers proudly carry their Dooney-Burk purses, dab on Calvin Klein perfume, admire the fit of their Tommy Hilfiger shirts and jeans, adjust their Oakley sunglasses, check the time on their Rolex watches, and sign the credit charge with their Mont Blanc pens. You are what you own, and these consumers are oozing with success. The only problem is this: all the status products could be fakes, counterfeits of the real thing that consumers willingly and knowingly buy.

Products provide not only a functional value, but a symbolic value as well. Ownership of branded status products communicate the owner's status to the world. Products have status because they are rare and highly desired, and this usually means they are expensive. Counterfeit products provide consumers the opportunity to own status goods at a price substantially lower than the going market price. Fakes are often inferior (purses that are not well made or shirts that are ruined when laundered) and may even be dangerous (sunglasses without UV tinting or perfume contaminated with bacteria), but there is a growing consumer demand for fake goods.

Fakes are better
than the
real thing.

SOCIAL MOBILITY

Social mobility, or the ability to move up or down the social hierarchy, also varies among societies. The social class boundaries in India, known as the caste system, are virtually impermeable to social mobility. People remain in the social class into which they are born.

In contrast, social mobility is a very real possibility in the United States, known as "the land of opportunity," "gold mountain," the place where anyone can grow up to be president, and a country replete with Horatio Alger stories, as captured in the illustration on p. 83. Education and occupation are the chief avenues to social mobility, followed by marriage.

Horatio Alger is
alive and well.

SPENDING IN CONFIDENCE

In 1998, consumers spent more than they earned. This milestone hasn't occurred since the Great Depression. Going into debt during the Great Depression was understandable and expected. In 1998, however, the motivator for consumers to spend more than they earned was called "irrational exuberance" —superhigh levels of consumer confidence that the economy is healthy and will continue to perform well. The consumer's psychological state has an influence on whether to save or spend. Consumers spend, go into debt, and deplete their savings when they are optimistic and feel good about the economy. On the other hand, consumers choose to pay off debt, save, and reduce or eliminate purchases of luxury and discretionary goods when they lack confidence in the

Ours is a country replete with Horatio Alger stories.

economy. Consumers spend when they are sunning in optimism and save when it is raining pessimism. The consumer sector accounts for two-thirds of the U.S. Gross National Product. Consumer confidence is a factor to be considered seriously.

Spending to debt.

GENERATIONS

DEMOGRAPHICS AND DESTINY

People who are members of the same generation (or *cohort* as sociologists call them) are more similar to each other than to members of other generations. Cohorts share similar life experiences and so tend to perceive the world in a similar fashion, share similar ages and stages in the life cycle, and so have similar needs and earning potential.

Arguably, demographics is not destiny. However, being a member of a given generation does have tremendous influence on the member's consumer behavior, and the collective action of a given generation has significant effects on the economy. Being a member of a large generation makes life crowded and competitive for its members, but the cohorts of that generation wield tremendous economic clout. Being a member of a small generation may provide a life of the pampered few; however, when such a small group roars, it may not be heard.

SENIORS RULE

- *Factoid:* Seniors will be 20% of the population by 2025.
- *Factoid:* By the year 2020, Americans over 65 will outnumber teenagers by a ratio of 2 to 1.
- *Factoid:* Because of the difference in life expectancy between men and women, an aging population means more women.
- *Factoid:* Seniors control 55% of the discretionary income in the United States.
- *Factoid:* Centenarians are the fastest-rising age group in the United States.
- *Factoid:* The AARP (American Association of Retired Persons) is one of the strongest special-interest groups in the United States.
- *Factoid:* The Great Depression and World War II left indelible marks on this generation.

This means that there are going to be a lot of grumpy old men and women (but mostly women) who have a lot of money to spend any way they want (but being financially and socially conservative, they won't be doing anything too crazy), who are politically savvy and who are going to be seniors longer than they are anything else (like teenagers or middle-agers).

CAN YOU READ THIS?

Type style, size, and density affect readability.

Following are some examples of type styles, sizes, and density:

This serif font can be easy to read, but only if it's large enough.

This compressed style is large enough, but somewhat crowded.

ALL CAPITALS CAN CREATE A TOO-BUSY EFFECT THAT'S HARD ON THE EYES, ESPECIALLY IN LENGTHY COPY THAT EXTENDS FOR TWO OR MORE LINES.

```
This clear, large, and loose style is easy on
eyes of all ages. However, it may not be the
most practical choice for all purposes be-
cause of space issues.
```

SOURCE: Guidelines proposed by Primelife, Inc., Orange, CA, and Age Wave, Inc., Emery, CA.

As people age, they have a harder time distinguishing blues and greens, things are not as bright, and small print (below 9 point) is virtually impossible to read. It's not just the size of the font, but the style of the font that must be considered. Some font styles are more difficult to read than others. Font size and style on product labels and store signage need to be designed so that they are visible to the senior-age target market.

As people age, they have a harder time bending and stretching to reach things. Products targeted for seniors should be placed in easy-to-reach locations so seniors do not have a great deal of stretching over their heads or bending below their knees to reach them.

Detroit recognizes the power of seniors. The Lincoln Town Car has two sets of radio and temperature controls. One set on the dashboard and one on the steering wheel make it easier for senior drivers to readjust their attention to the road after fiddling with the controls. Chrysler has electromagnetic rear-view mirrors that automatically dim the reflection of headlights. Mercedes has introduced anti-glare halogen headlamps.[7]

> Just like in high school, seniors rule.

BOOMERS (THE GENERATION BORN BETWEEN 1946 AND 1964)

- *Factoid:* Boomers make up 30% of the current population.
- *Factoid:* Boomers have a combined income of $985 billion.
- *Factoid:* Boomers grew up in the bountiful post-war period.
- *Factoid:* The Boomer's battle cry in college was, "Don't trust anyone over 30."
- *Factoid:* Boomers are the first generation to send record numbers of women into the workforce.
- *Factoid:* Boomer hippies wanted to redefine social boundaries.

Seniors may rule, but Boomers are the two-ton elephant. The sheer size and economic power of this group demand that marketers cater to their changing life-cycle needs. Boomers define the meaning of the life-stage they occupy. If 77 million people say that forty-something is not old, then forty-something is not old. If they say "Grandpa" Mick Jagger of the Rolling Stones is hot, then he's hot. If they say Tina Turner can still strut her stuff on those gorgeous, shapely legs, who are you to argue with 77 million people? This generation feels entitled to a world that will be shaped to their expectations.

Harry S. Dent, Jr., author of the book *The Great Boom Ahead*, goes so far as to suggest that the current robust economy owes much to the boomers who began moving into their peak years of earning (and investing and spending) beginning in the late 1980s. For Dent, the epiphany that baby boomers are responsible for the economy occurred when he charted the U.S. population trends and the stock market and realized that both looked "like the same chart with a 45-year lag."[8]

Products age with the boomers. By using elastic waistbands and a bit of Lycra, Levis, the boomers' second skin, can mature with the boomers. Generous, "casual" styles try to accommodate the less-firm thighs and rear ends.

> Follow them to their graves.

The size and buying power of this generation demands marketers attend constantly to their changing needs as they progress through their life cycle.

GENERATION X (THE GENERATION BORN BETWEEN 1965 AND 1976)

■ *Factoid:* Generation X (or Gen X) grew up with technology.

■ *Factoid:* Gen X is taking the slow road to maturity, taking longer to graduate from college, taking longer to enter into real jobs (career positions), living at home with mom and dad longer, marrying at an older age (if at all), and having children at a later age (if at all).

■ *Factoid:* Gen X grew up watching a lot of television and is a media-savvy group.

■ *Factoid:* Generation X got its name from Douglas Coupland's book[9] of the same name.

■ *Factoid:* Gen X is the smallest generation, sandwiched between the two largest—boomers and the echo boom.

■ *Factoid:* Fully one-third of the members of this generation are minorities.[10,11]

Here is a humorous glimpse from the world of Generation X.[12]

404 Clueless. From the World Wide Web error message "404—Not Found," meaning that the requested document could not be located. "Don't bother asking him—he's 404, man."

Alpha Geek The most knowledgeable, technically proficient person in an office or work group. "Ask Larry, he's the alpha geek around here."

Adminisphere The rarefied organizational layers beginning just above the rank and file. Decisions that fall from the adminisphere are often profoundly inappropriate or irrelevant to the problems they were designed to solve.

Assmosis The process that some people use to attain success and advancement (i.e., kissing up to the boss). You will all be measured on this at some point in your career.

Beepilepsy The brief seizure people sometimes suffer when their beepers go off, especially in vibrator mode. Beepilepsy is characterized by physical spasms, goofy facial expressions, and stopping speech in mid-sentence.

Blamestorming Sitting around in a group discussing why a deadline was missed, why a project failed, and who was responsible.

Body Nazis Hardcore exercise and weight-lifting fanatics who look down on anyone who doesn't work out obsessively.

Brain Fart A byproduct of a bloated mind producing information effortlessly. A burst of useful information. "I know you're busy on the Microsoft story, but can you give us a brain fart on the Mitnik bust?" Variation of old hacker slang that had more negative connotations.

CGI Joe A hardcore CGI script programmer who has all the social skills and charisma of a plastic action figure.

Chainsaw Consultant   An outside expert brought in to reduce the employee head count and leave the brass with clean hands.

CLM (Career Limiting Move)   Used among microserfs to describe ill-advised activity. Trashing your boss while he or she is within earshot is a serious CLM. (Also known as CLB [Career Limiting Behavior])

Cobweb Site   A World Wide Web Site that hasn't been updated for a long time. A dead web page.

Cube Farm   An office filled with cubicles.

Dead Tree Edition   The paper version of a publication available in both paper and electronic forms." Do you have the dead tree edition of the *San Francisco Chronicle*?"

Dilberted   To be exploited and oppressed by your boss. Derived from the experiences of Dilbert, the geek-in-hell comic-strip character. "I've been dilberted again. The old man revised the specs for the fourth time this week."

Dorito Syndrome   Feelings of emptiness and dissatisfaction triggered by addictive substances that lack nutritional content. "I just spent six hours surfing the Web, and now I've got a bad case of Dorito syndrome."

Ego Surfing   Scanning the Internet, databases, print media, and so on, looking for references to one's own name.

Elvis Year   The peak year of something's or someone's popularity. "Barney the Dinosaur's Elvis year was 1993."

Flight Risk   Used to describe employees who are suspected of planning to leave the company or department soon.

Glazing   Corporatespeak for sleeping with your eyes open. A popular pastime at conferences and early-morning meetings. "Didn't he notice that half the room was glazing by the second session?"

Gray Matter   Older, experienced business people hired by young entrepreneurial firms looking to appear more reputable and established.

Graybar Land   The place you go while you're staring at a computer that's processing something very slowly (while you watch the gray bar creep across the screen). "I was in graybar land for what seemed like hours, thanks to that CAD rendering."

Idea Hamsters   People who always seem to have their idea generators running.

It's a Feature   From the adage, "It's not a bug, it's a feature." Used sarcastically to describe an unpleasant experience that you wish to gloss over.

Keyboard Plaque   The disgusting buildup of dirt and crud found on computer keyboards.

Mouse Potato   The online, wired generation's answer to the couch potato.

Ohnosecond   That minuscule fraction of time in which you realize that you've just made a BIG mistake.

Open-Collar Workers   People who work at home or who telecommute.

Percussive Maintenance   The fine art of whacking an electronic device to get it to work again.

Perot   To quit unexpectedly."My cellular phone just perot'ed."

Prairie Dogging   When someone yells or drops something loudly in a "cube farm," and people's heads pop up over the walls to see what's going on.

Seagull Manager   A manager who flies in, makes a lot of noise, poops on everything, and then leaves.

Salmon Day   The experience of spending an entire day swimming upstream only to get screwed and die in the end.

SITCOMs   What yuppies turn into when they have children and one of them stops working to stay home with the kids (acronym for Single Income, Two Children, Oppressive Mortgage).

Squirt the Bird   To transmit a signal up to a satellite. "Crew and talent are ready—what time do we squirt the bird?"

Starter Marriage   A short-lived first marriage that ends in divorce with no kids, no property, and no regrets.

Stress Puppy   A person who seems to thrive on being stressed out and whiny.

Swiped Out   An ATM or credit card that has been rendered useless because the magnetic strip is worn away from extensive use.

Tourists   People who take training classes just to get a vacation from their jobs. "We had three serious students in the class; the rest were just tourists."

Treeware   Hacker slang for documentation or other printed material.

Uninstalled   Euphemism for being fired.

Under Mouse Arrest   Getting busted for violating an on-line service provider's rule of conduct. "Sorry I couldn't get back to you. AOL put me under mouse arrest."

World Wide Wait   The real meaning of WWW.

Xerox Subsidy   Euphemism for swiping free photocopies from one's workplace.

THE STORY OF X

Gen X'ers—a small generational group sandwiched between two larger groups—engage in X-treme sports, read X-men comics, watch the *X-Files* television show, grew up listening to the band Xene, know about the dangers of prolonged exposure to X-rays and X-rated movies, have never heard of carbon paper but take Xerox machines for granted, are a generation so multicultural and multi-ethnic that there is little chance of Xenophobia, and grew up receiving computers, CDs, video games, and other technological wonders for Xmas. They are a generation coming of age and will provide the political and business leadership in the ensuing years.

> X marks
> their spot.

Gen Y, Fruit of the Boom (ages 5 to 22)[10]

- *Factoid:* This generation is about as large as the boomer generation.
- *Factoid:* Gen Y is even more technologically savvy than Gen X. Gen Y grew up on the Web.
- *Factoid:* This is a sophisticated, consuming generation. One out of nine high school students has a credit card co-signed by a parent.
- *Factoid:* This is the most ethnically diverse generation. One out of three is a minority.
- *Factoid:* One out of four members of Gen Y grew up in a single-parent family.
- *Factoid:* Mom at work is the norm. Three out of four come from homes with full-time working mothers.

Generation Y, also called the "baby echo" or the "baby boomlet," grew up with the computer mouse in hand, had access to over 100 cable stations, is looking forward to Web TV and high definition TV, and views the microwave oven as a standard kitchen appliance like the refrigerator and stove.

Gen Y started shopping at much earlier age and has been a serious source of input into family decisions from family vacations to type of car to buy. The sophisticated consumer behavior of this generation means that they still like traditional kid goods, but for a shorter amount of time. Not good news for Mattel's Barbie doll.

Members of Gen Y want food not only to be tasty but interactive and fun. Kids love candies that are gross and disgusting. It's fun to eat boogers, chomp on eyeballs, and chew on gummy rats. This is even more appealing because adults would gag at the prospect of eating these candies.

For example, consider the appeal of Good Humor–Breyers's Tongue Splashers. The product features a blue tongue protruding from an open mouth with a dangling tonsil. Stuck onto the blue tongue is a gumball that upon first chomp will explode and color your mouth in awesome hues. To boomer parents, Good Humor–Breyers's Tongue Splashers may be somewhat reminiscent of the Rolling Stones' logo on a stick; to the fruit of the boom, however, it is "way cool." A multicolored, dyed mouth is a dead giveaway that the person has eaten a Tongue Splashers.[13]

To boomers, Good Humor–Breyers's Tongue Splashers may be somewhat reminiscent of the Rolling Stones' logo on a stick; to the fruit of the boom, however, it's just "way cool!"

LIKE FATHER, LIKE SON . . . NOT![14]

Generation Y likes nostalgia, just like their boomer parents, but whereas boomers look longingly back on the nostalgic good old days, Gen Y treats the nostalgic good old days as a huge treasure chest from which to pick and choose items, styles, and appearances that personalize their unique sense of self. Members of Gen Y want to be members but adopt a "my way" culture. This is fueled by the Internet, which allows for and encourages the growth of diversity (contrary to television, which is a more homogenizing medium). The medium of choice for boomers is the television, but for their children it is the Internet.

Gen Y is not like its boomer parents. Belatedly, Levis discovered that Gen Y's definition of baggy-fitting jeans does not mean the "casual fitting" jeans that their parents wear, and Nike discovered that Gen Y would "Just Do It" in hiking boots—not in tennis shoes (their parents' choice). Advertisements that use humor, irony, and truth seem to be effective with Gen Y.

Y, because they are a huge market.

9

CULTURE

HOW DO YOU KNOW IF YOU'RE WET OR NOT WHEN YOU'RE UNDER WATER?

UNIVERSAL FACIAL EXPRESSIONS

Facial expressions are universal communicators. There are commonalities of facial expressions among people of different cultures. A smile is the most universal common communicator.[1]

In Japan you can attend "smile schools," 90-minute, weekly classes that teach the Japanese people how to smile more. Successful modern business practice requires the establishment of friendly personal relationships. In a country where tradition encourages the repression of emotions, attendance at smile schools may actually improve the country's bottom line.[2]

In their fascinating book *Emotional Contagion,* Rapson, Hatfield, and Cacioppo[3] present the intriguing finding that when you smile in response to another person's smile, it actually lifts your spirits. We smile when we are happy, but smiling can also make us happy. Emotions can be inside out (you are happy so you smile) and outside in, too (you smile and that makes you a bit happier).

Smile a lot.

CULTURE IS EVOLUTIONARY

During World War II, the V was the American victory sign. During the 1960s hippie era, the V was a peace sign. The highly visible Mercedes-Benz logo was the peace symbol during the hippie era of the 1960s.

Nonverbal communication changes meaning over time.

YOU DIDN'T MEAN TO SAY THAT

The cover of a greeting card shows a picture of a hand with a "thumbs up" sign. Upon opening the card, the recipient reads, "Way to go!" This is a congratulations card. The thumbs-up sign in the United States is a positive communication. In Northern Sardina, the thumbs-up sign is an obscene gesture.

CHAPTER 9 ■ HOW DO YOU KNOW IF YOU'RE WET OR NOT WHEN YOU'RE UNDER WATER?

92

	Percentage Agreement in How Photograph Was Judged Across Cultures				
	UNITED STATES (J=99)	BRAZIL (J=40)	CHILE (J=119)	ARGEN- TINA (J=168)	JAPAN (J=29)
Fear	85%	67%	68%	54%	66%
Disgust	92%	97%	92%	92%	90%
Happiness	97%	95%	95%	98%	100%
Anger	67%	90%	94%	90%	90%

These pictures show the commonality of facial expressions of people in different countries.

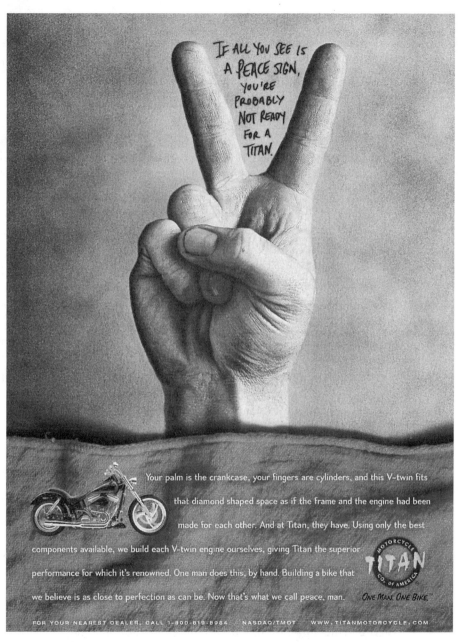

This advertisement for Harley-Davidson Motorcycles captures
the evolutionary meaning of the "V" sign.

Another greeting card shows a hand forming the OK sign. In the United States it communicates that things are going well. In Southern Greece, the OK sign is used to call someone an uncomplimentary part of the anatomy.

CHAPTER 9 ■ HOW DO YOU KNOW IF YOU'RE WET OR NOT WHEN YOU'RE UNDER WATER?

94

THAT ISN'T WHAT THEY MEANT TO SAY

Each language has its peculiar idiomatic expressions, slang, nuances, and twists. As the examples that follow show, humorous translation errors have occurred.[4]

In a Paris hotel elevator: PLEASE LEAVE YOUR VALUES AT THE FRONT DESK.

In a hotel in Athens: VISITORS ARE EXPECTED TO COMPLAIN AT THE OFFICE BETWEEN THE HOURS OF 9 AND 11 A.M. DAILY.

In a Japanese hotel: YOU ARE INVITED TO TAKE ADVANTAGE OF THE CHAMBERMAID.

In the lobby of a Moscow hotel across from a Russian Orthodox monastery: YOU ARE WELCOME TO VISIT THE CEMETERY WHERE FAMOUS RUSSIAN AND SOVIET COMPOSERS, ARTISTS AND WRITERS ARE BURIED DAILY EXCEPT THURSDAY.

On the menu of a Swiss restaurant: OUR WINES LEAVE YOU NOTHING TO HOPE FOR.

Outside a Hong Kong tailor shop: LADIES MAY HAVE A FIT UPSTAIRS.

Outside a Paris dress shop: DRESSES FOR STREET WALKING.

In an advertisement by a Hong Kong dentist: TEETH EXTRACTED BY THE LATEST METHODIST.

In a Rome laundry: LADIES, LEAVE YOUR CLOTHES HERE AND SPEND THE AFTERNOON HAVING A GOOD TIME.

In a Copenhagen airline ticket office: WE TAKE YOUR BAGS AND SEND THEM IN ALL DIRECTIONS.

On the door of a Moscow hotel room: IF THIS IS YOUR FIRST VISIT TO THE USSR, YOU ARE WELCOME TO IT.

At a Budapest zoo: PLEASE DO NOT FEED THE ANIMALS. IF YOU HAVE ANY SUITABLE FOOD, GIVE IT TO THE GUARD ON DUTY.

In the office of a Roman doctor: SPECIALIST IN WOMEN AND OTHER DISEASES.

In an Acapulco hotel: THE MANAGER HAS PERSONALLY PASSED ALL THE WATER SERVED HERE.

THAT ISN'T WHAT I MEANT TO SAY

As the translation blunders below illustrate, it's not that easy to translate American English to other languages.[5]

Coor's Light—"Turn it loose tonight" became "Have the runs tonight" in Spanish.

Perdue chicken—"It takes a tough man to make a tender chicken" became "It takes a sexually excited man to make a chicken affectionate" in Spanish.

"Bichos" means bugs to Mexicans, but to Puerto Ricans it refers to a man's private parts. Consequently, an insecticide ad that claims to kill bichos left Puerto Ricans puzzled.

Colgate marketed its Cue toothpaste in France, not knowing that "cue" is a slang pornographic term.

TABLE 9.1	BRITISH "ENGLISH" WORDS	
1. Pram	2. Nappy	3. Solicitor
4. Pillar box	5. Lorry	6. Smalls
7. Turf accountant	8. Gangway	9. Sweet
10. Lift	11. Let	12. Fortnight
13. Torch	14. Wireless	15. Trunk call
16. Bum	17. Loo	18. Lolly
19. Dabs	20. Boot	21. Bonnet
22. Jello	23. Biscuit	

American "English" equivalent: 1. Baby carriage, 2. Diaper, 3. Lawyer, 4. Mail box, 5. Truck, 6. Underwear, 7. Bookie, 8. Aisle, 9. Dessert, 10. Elevator, 11. Rent (lease), 12. Two weeks, 13. Flashlight, 14. Radio, 15. Long distance, 16. Butt, 17. Bathroom, 18. Money, 19. Fingerprints, 20. Trunk (of a car), 21. Hood (of a car), 22. Jam or jelly, 23. Crackers.

TABLE 9.2	AUSTRALIAN "ENGLISH" WORDS	
1. Ankle biter	2. Boomer	3. Cheese and kisses
4. Earbasher	5. Pokies	6. Sheila
7. Grasshopper	8. Tomato sauce	9. Amber fluid
10. Brolly	11. Chrissie	12. Jumper
13. Sanger	14. Strides	15. Mozzie

American Equivalent: 1. Small child, 2. Kangaroo, 3. Wife, 4. Bore, 5. Slot machines, 6. Young women, 7. Tourist, 8. Ketchup, 9. Beer, 10. Umbrella, 11. Christmas, 12. Sweater, 13. Sandwich, 14. Men's pants, 15. Mosquito.

> Laundry detergent advertised as especially effective for the "dirty parts" of the wash became especially effective for one's "private parts" when translated in French-speaking Quebec.

ENGLISH IS NOT ALWAYS ENGLISH[6]

Winston Churchill said that America and England are "two great peoples separated by a common language."

In England a movie that is a bomb is a success. In the United States, a movie that is a bomb is a failure. Try to guess the American English equivalent of the British English words listed in Table 9.1.

Try to identify the American English equivalent of the Australian English words listed in Table 9.2.

An effective way to avoid translation blunders is to use back translation. Have a person translate the statements from one language (English) to another language (French), and then have another person translate back (from French to English). Make sure the translations are equivalent.

Use back translation to avoid blunders.

CHAPTER 9 ■ HOW DO YOU KNOW IF YOU'RE WET OR NOT WHEN YOU'RE UNDER WATER?

96

TABLE 9.3	APPROPRIATE AND INAPPROPRIATE GIFTS AROUND THE WORLD			
China	**India**	**Japan**	**Mexico**	**Saudi Arabia**
Appropriate Gifts				
Modest gifts such as coffee table books, ties, pens	Sweets, nuts, fruit, elephant carvings, candle holders	Scotch, brandy, Americana, round fruit such as melons	Desk clocks, fine pens, gold lighters	Fine compasses to determine direction for prayer, cashmere
Inappropriate Gifts				
Clocks, anything from Taiwan	Leather objects, snake images	Gifts that come in quantities of 4 or 9	Sterling silver items, logo gifts, food baskets	Pork, pigskin, liquor

GIFT OR GAFFE?[7]

Gifts are gestures and symbols of appreciation, welcome, or gratitude. To prevent a gift from becoming an embarrassing gaffe, the gift giver must be aware what the culture of a country defines as appropriate or inappropriate. When in Japan, never give gifts that come in sets of four or nine. They are considered unlucky numbers. On the other hand, nine is a lucky number to the Chinese; in fact, they have been known to bid hundreds—even thousands—of dollars for the privilege of having the numbers nine or eight (another lucky number) appear on their car license plates. However, giving a timepiece is symbolic of an end to a relationship and offends the Chinese. On the other hand, clocks would be appropriate gifts in Mexico.

TICK TOCK: THE PACE OF LIFE[8,9]

Time is measured differently in different cultures. In American culture, as well as other industrialized nations, time is linear. Linear time can be allocated into chunks, such as work time and leisure time. Time is analogous to money and like money, it can be saved and spent.

Other cultures have vastly different views of time. American Indians, for example, have procedural time. How long it takes to get something done is however long it takes something to get done. In cultures with circular time, time is viewed as the passage of natural-occurring events like sunrise, sunset, and the changing seasons.

The pace of life varies among different countries and also among different regions in the United States, as illustrated in Table 9.4. Adaptation to a different culture includes adaptation to the pace of life. The pace of life may be so fast that it makes a new arrival nervous, or the pace of life may be so slow that a new arrival finds himself unreasonably impatient.

| TABLE 9.4 | RANK OF 31 COUNTRIES FOR OVERALL PACE OF LIFE AND FOR THREE RELATED MEASURES: MINUTES DOWNTOWN PEDESTRIANS TAKE TO WALK 60 FEET; MINUTES IT TAKES A POSTAL CLERK TO COMPLETE A STAMP PURCHASE TRANSACTION; AND ACCURACY (IN MINUTES) OF PUBLIC CLOCKS |

Country	Overall Pace of Life	Walking 60 feet	Postal Service	Public Clock
Switzerland	1	3	2	1
Ireland	2	1	3	11
Germany	3	5	1	8
Japan	4	7	4	6
Italy	5	10	12	2
England	6	4	9	13
Sweden	7	13	5	7
Austria	8	23	8	3
Netherlands	9	2	14	25
Hong Kong	10	14	6	14
France	11	8	18	10
Poland	12	12	15	8
Costa Rica	13	16	10	15
Taiwan	14	18	7	21
Singapore	15	25	11	4
United States	16	6	23	20
Canada	17	11	21	22
South Korea	18	20	20	16
Hungary	19	19	19	18
Czech Republic	20	21	17	23
Greece	21	14	13	29
Kenya	22	9	30	24
China	23	24	25	12
Bulgaria	24	27	22	17
Romania	25	30	29	5
Jordan	26	28	27	19
Syria	27	29	28	27
El Salvador	28	22	16	31
Brazil	29	31	24	28
Indonesia	30	26	26	30
Mexico	31	17	31	26

SOURCE: Robert Levine.

TORTOISE WINS

Among 36 U.S. cities, fast-paced places usually have higher rates of heart disease (see Table 9.5).

In the United States more than fifteen minutes may be considered unreasonably late for a business meeting. In Latin American cultures, the definition of unreasonably late is substantially longer. The pace of life is an invisible, intangible regulator that pervades and defines the rhythm of a culture.

Culture is the measure of time.

CHAPTER 9 ■ HOW DO YOU KNOW IF YOU'RE WET OR NOT WHEN YOU'RE UNDER WATER?

98

TABLE 9.5	Top Ten Cities Ranked by Walking Speed of Pedestrians, Talking Speed of Postal Clerks, Percent of Adults Wearing Wristwatches, and Rate of Coronary Heart Disease			
Fast Walkers	**Fast Talkers**	**Watch Wearers**	**Coronaries**
Springfield, MA	Columbus, OH	New York, NY	New York, NY
Boston, MA	Atlanta, GA	Boston, MA	Buffalo, NY
Atlanta, GA	Chicago, IL	Detroit, MI	Providence, RI
Salt Lake City, UT	Youngstown, OH	Buffalo, NY	Worchester, MA
Buffalo, NY	Bakersfield, CA	San Francisco, CA	Patterson, NJ
Kansas City, MO	Worchester, MA	Worchester, MA	Youngstown, OH
Providence, RI	Boston, MA	Rochester, NY	Springfield, MA
Nashville, TN	Indianapolis, IN	Oxnard, CA	St. Louis, MO
Worchester, MA	Providence, RI	San Diego, CA	Canton, OH
Houston, TX	St. Louis, MO	Salt Lake City, UT	Boston, MA

SOURCE: Robert Levine.

The increasing ethnic diversity is redefining the American cultural definition of beauty. A contemporary beauty such as supermodel Tyson Beckford doesn't look much like a model you would find in magazines in the 50s, 60s, 70s, or 80s.

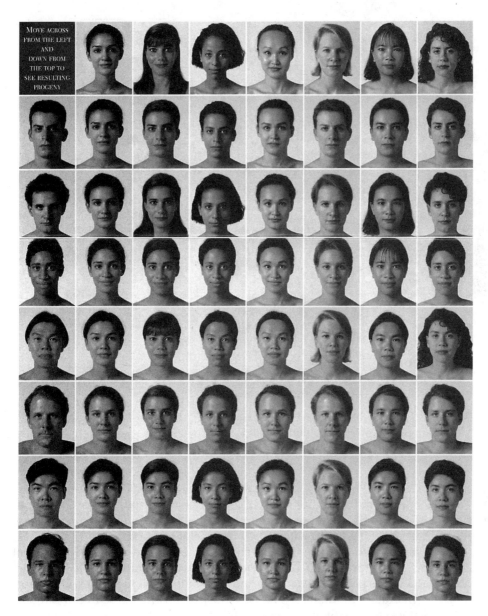

Beautiful ethnic blends. This computer-generated photograph shows children of parents from mixed ethnic backgrounds. The first row and first column are "parents." The cell intersection of a woman in the first row with a man in the first column is their "offspring."

THE DIVERSIFICATION OF THE AMERICAN CULTURE

Each generation is experiencing a greater ethnic and cultural diversity than the preceding one. This is reflected in many ways in our daily lives.

CHAPTER 9 ■ HOW DO YOU KNOW IF YOU'RE WET OR NOT WHEN YOU'RE UNDER WATER?

100

A thoroughly modern Betty Crocker has evolved over the years, from "Home Economist Betty" in 1936 (far left) to "Mother Betty" in 1955 (top) to "Power Betty" in 1985 (far right). Now the most recent Betty Crocker is an amalgam of the ethnic diversity of the United States. She is "Multicultural Betty" (bottom).

Pass the salsa, and hold the catsup. Salsa sales have surpassed the sale of catsup. Americans have the opportunity to savor the richness and textures of food from all corners of the world within their own neighborhoods.

Diversity changes marketing demands and opportunities.

The increasing ethnic diversity is redefining the sizing norms. The current "well baby" charts for children under two are based on a sample of 867 Caucasian, formula-fed babies born between 1929 and 1975 in the Yellow Springs, Ohio, area to largely middle-class families. The new standard will be based on a national sample that is reflective of the increased ethnic diversity.[10]

THE SAME FOOD TASTES DIFFERENT IN OTHER COUNTRIES

Pizza is a favorite food in the United States. Pizza is consumed in other countries as well. But if you were to order pizza in other countries, you might find toppings other than the U.S. favorite, pepperoni: In England, tuna and corn; in Japan, squid and fish; in Guatamala, black bean sauce.[11]

Dunkin' Donuts sells both salty chicken and cheese donuts in Brazil. McDonald's developed a beefless Big Mac for Hindus in India who do not eat beef. In Japan, apples are more pink than red. Red apples look unnatural to the Japanese, and their shiny quality makes them think about the poisoned apples in Snow White. In Japan Oreos have no filling. To the Japanese palette, Oreos with filling are too sweet.[12,13]

> Culture teaches consumers the meaning of products, their uses, and their value.

HUMOR MAY BE CULTURE SPECIFIC

The advertisement below is humorous in the context of the American culture. A rabbit holding a human foot would not be funny to consumers not familiar with American culture.

A rabbit holding a human foot is humorous only if the consumer understands that a rabbit's foot is considered a lucky charm in the American culture.

CHAPTER 9 ■ HOW DO YOU KNOW IF YOU'RE WET OR NOT WHEN YOU'RE UNDER WATER?

102

CONSUMER GOODS ACQUIRE MEANING FROM CULTURAL RITUALS

A birthday celebration means a cake with candles, presents, and maybe funny hats or noisemakers. Easter includes egg hunts for children. Halloween would not be Halloween without costumes and trick-or-treating. These events are cultural rituals. They occur periodically and predictably. The behavior patterns associated with them are sequenced and have symbolic meanings.

Apart from cultural rituals, individuals may have their own. These rituals often involve consumer goods. Before a big exam, Bob always attempts to get seven and one-half hours of sleep. For breakfast, he will make two fried eggs sunny side up and two strips of bacon. He lays the eggs and bacon out so that it reads one hundred and a smile. That is the grade he will earn on his exam!

HOW THE SACRED BECOMES PROFANE

The Statue of Liberty is a symbol of hope, opportunity, and freedom to millions of people and is cherished and valued by its citizens. The millions of tourists who visit the statue can buy a souvenir of it. On sale are Statue of Liberty cigarette lighters, pencil sharpeners, can openers, pins, refrigerator magnets, and tee-shirts. Consumers can even buy and wear silly-looking Statue of Liberty sponge crowns. The abundant availability and variety of Statue of Liberty insignia goods causes it to lose some of its sacredness.

The mysterious and captivating smile of the Mona Lisa has been a subject of interest to art scholars. It is considered an icon of feminine beauty. However, television commercials featuring the Mona Lisa with a talking mouth and advertisements showing her wearing a "Breathe Right" patch erase the aura of mystery that surrounds the painting.

HOW THE PROFANE BECOMES SACRED

Ordinary things can take on special meaning to mark a significant event or association with special (sacred) persons or places. For example, reports of Elvis sightings notwithstanding, the king is dead. Since his death, Elvis memorabilia has become sacred for the millions of devoted, and people make pilgrimages to Graceland, Elvis's home. The following is a spoof that provides a humorous interpretation of the similarities between Elvis and Jesus.[14]

Jesus	Elvis
Jesus H. Christ has 12 letters.	Elvis Presley has 12 letters.
Jesus was part of the trinity.	Elvis's first band was a trio.
Jesus walked on water. (Matthew 14:25)	Elvis surfed. (*Blue Hawaii*, 1966)
Jesus was a carpenter.	Elvis took wood shop and industrial arts in high school.

Jesus is the Lord's Shepherd.	Elvis dated Cybill Shepherd.
Jesus said, "Love thy neighbor." (Matthew 22:39)	Elvis said, "Don't be Cruel." (RCA, 1956)
Jesus is a Capricorn (December 25)	Elvis is a Capricorn (January 8).
Jesus' countenance was like lightning. (Matthew 28:3)	Elvis's trademarks were a lightning bolt and snow-white jumpsuits.
Mary had an Immaculate Conception.	Priscilla went to Immaculate Conception High School.
Jesus fasted for 40 days and nights.	Elvis had irregular eating habits.
Jesus was Jewish.	Elvis was part Jewish (great-grandmother).
Jesus was resurrected.	Elvis had a comeback in 1968.
Jesus' Father is everywhere.	Elvis's father, Vernon, was a drifter who moved around quite a bit.

SOURCE: Michael R. Solomon, http://auburn.edu/solommr.

THE CONSUMER DECISION PROCESS
LOGICAL, RATIONAL DECISION MAKING . . . NOT!

BE A PEACH AMONG LEMONS

Real estate agents will sometimes purposely show clients several homes that they know their clients will not like before they show the home that they think their clients probably will like. Dragging clients around to several unappealing homes first will make the appealing home even more attractive.

Sometimes you win a promotion not because you are good but because the others are so bad. Sometimes you become the committee chair not because you took a step forward, but because everyone else took a step backward.

Sometimes comparing your product to inferior competitors will be more advantageous than aligning your product to superior or comparable competitors. Placing your more expensive, discontinued computer model next to your new, less expensive and more versatile computer model highlights the better price, versatility, and other advantages of the new model.

> Be thankful for inferiors. Inferiors make you look superior.

GOLDILOCKS AND THE THREE BEARS

In the children's fairy tale, Goldilocks tries Papa Bear's porridge and determines that it is too cold, Mama Bear's porridge is too hot, but Baby's Bear's porridge is just right. When she tries Papa Bear's bed, she discovers that it is too hard, Mama Bear's bed is too soft, but Baby Bear's bed is just right.

Consumers shy away from extremes. Present consumers with a choice of alternatives, anchored by a very expensive model on one end and a very inexpensive model on the other. The expensive model offers too many never-to-be-used features and an unnecessarily high quality level. The inexpensive model does not offer enough features and the quality level is suspect, partially due to its too low price. Consumers will buy the moderately priced model. By anchoring the moderately priced model with these extremes, many more will be sold than by offering the moderately priced model alone.

> Be baby bear.

FRAMES ARE NOT JUST FOR PAINTINGS

Your child comes home with her first oil painting. It is not a Rembrandt. You notice that the perspective is off and the colors are not quite right, but you are very proud of it and hang it on the wall. One day you decide that the painting could use a frame. So you and your daughter take the painting to a frame store to have it framed. You are floored by the price, having had no idea that frames cost so much. But your daughter is beaming. You relent and let her pick out the frame. Home again, you hang the painting back on the wall. Instantly you are amazed. The painting looks so much better. The right frame, you realize, can make a big difference.

Frame your offerings.

Marketers can benefit by framing their offers. It's better to inform customers that paying in cash will save them 2.5 percent than it is to inform them that using credit cards will cost them 2.5 percent more. Labeling hamburger as 75 percent lean is a better than labeling the hamburger as 25 percent fat.[1,2,3]

CONSUMER DECISION RULES "RULE"[4]

Do consumers select characteristics and then compare brands based on those characteristics, or do they consider brands, one at a time, on a number of selected characteristics? That is, do brands come first or do product characteristics come first? But does this really make any difference? Yes, sometimes.

How do consumers buy computers? Do they look at all the Compaq computers, move on to the IBM computers, then mosey over to the Hewlett-Packard computers? If this is how consumers shop for computers, then retailers should group their product offerings by brand. On the other hand, if consumers shop for computers by consideration of price points, then the retailer should group computers by price, say those under $500, those $500 to $1,000, and those above $1,000.

Obey consumer-decision rules.

When consumers buy spices at the grocery store, do they care if they are buying spice, essence, flavoring, or extract? Or do they just want the thyme and rosemary for their Italian recipe? Taking the extra time and investing the extra labor to stock shelves by these brand characteristics—spice, essence, flavoring, and extract—is a waste of time and money if consumers don't consider these product characteristics in their decision making.

JUST THE FACTS, MA'AM

Economists will tell you that optimal decisions can be attained with more information. Consumers will tell you that more information sometimes leads to information overload and results in worse decisions. In such cases, consumers may not know which information is more relevant and may find that more information actually dilutes the quality of the decision. That is why publications such as *Consumer Reports* are so popular. As if responding to Detective Joe Friday's weary plea on the long-running television program *Dragnet, Consumer Reports* presents "just the facts, ma'am."

Dilution is not the solution.

"How To Fool Consumers" or "Caveat Emptor"?

Be Careful, It Can Be Dangerous Out There.

From the perspective of the unscrupulous marketer, this section can appropriately be titled, "How to Fool Consumers." From the perspective of consumers, an apt title for this section could be "Caveat Emptor," or let the buyer beware.

Word Games[1]

The art of selecting the right words will allow the marketer to say what he wants to say without actually saying it.

Implied superiority	"I cannot recommend this brand any higher."	*Interpretations:* Does this mean that this product was compared to all other brands and was deemed the best, or does it mean that after comparison to all the other brands, some brands were better, and this is the highest recommendation the rater could give it?
Juxtaposed imperative	"Make $10,000 a month working just 4 hours a day. Call 1-800-916-4262."	*Interpretations:* Readers are supposed to conclude that they can earn $10,000 a month working 4 hours a day if they call 800-916-4262. However, the ad does not state this. The reader arrives at this conclusion because the two statements are next to each other.

Incomplete comparison	"Excite Coffee. It's the best on the market."	*Interpretations*: The ad does not say how Excite Coffee is the best. Is it best in taste? Convenience? Value? Package design?
Multiple comparison	"County Hospital is more caring than General Hospital, requires less waiting than Memorial Hospital, and allows longer maternity stays than University Hospital."	*Interpretations:* The reader may conclude that County Hospital is superior to General Hospital, Memorial Hospital and University Hospital on all attributes. In actuality, the ad only claims that County Hospital is superior to the other hospitals on selected attributes.
Meaningless claims	"Lite olive oil" "Fat free"	*Interpretations:* Readers are supposed to conclude that this is a healthy product because it does not contain fat. What it doesn't say is that it may be loaded with calories from sugar.
	"Cholesterol free"	*Interpretations:* To proclaim that a vegetable product such as potato chips does not contain cholesterol is stating the obvious. Only animal products contain cholesterol. Consumers who may not know this are supposed to conclude that the product is healthy. However, the product may be high in salt and/or fat.

MORE WORD GAMES

The art of promising more than intended.

The marketing tactics listed above may be viewed as harboring "hidden agendas" or attempts to imply more than what is there, but what are the intentions of the following actual labels and instructions on consumer goods? The statements in parentheses are possible consumer reactions.[2]

On a Sears hairdryer: DO NOT USE WHILE SLEEPING.
(Gee, that's the only time I have to work on my hair!)

On a bag of Fritos: YOU COULD BE A WINNER! NO PURCHASE NECESSARY.
DETAILS INSIDE.
(The shoplifter special!)

On a bar of Dial soap: DIRECTIONS: USE LIKE REGLUAR SOAP.
(And that would be how?)

On some Swan frozen dinners: SERVING SUGGESTION: DEFROST.
(But it's *just* a suggestion!)

On a hotel-provided shower cap in a box: FITS ONE HEAD.

On Tesco's Tiramisu dessert (printed on bottom of the box): DO NOT TURN
UPSIDE DOWN.
(Too late! You lose!—I love it: food to piss you off.)

On Marks & Spencer Bread Pudding: PRODUCT WILL BE HOT AFTER HEATING.
(Are you sure? Let's experiment!)

On packaging for a Rowenta iron: DO NOT IRON CLOTHES ON BODY.
(But wouldn't that save more time? And by the way, whose body?)

On Boot's Children's cough medicine: DO NOT DRIVE CAR OR OPERATE MACHINERY.
(We could do a lot to reduce the rate of construction accidents if we just
kept medicated 5-year-olds off those forklifts.)

On Nytol sleep aid: WARNING: MAY CAUSE DROWSINESS.
(One would hope!)

On a Korean kitchen knife: WARNING: KEEP OUT OF CHILDREN.
(Or pets! What's for dinner?)

On a string of Chinese-made Christmas lights: FOR INDOOR OR OUTDOOR
USE ONLY.
(As opposed to use in outer space or underground.)

On a Japanese food processor: NOT TO BE USED FOR THE OTHER USE.
(Now I'm curious.)

On Sainsbury's peanuts: WARNING: CONTAINS NUTS.

On an American Airlines packet of nuts: INSTRUCTIONS: OPEN PACKET, EAT NUTS.

On a Swedish chainsaw: DO NOT ATTEMPT TO STOP CHAIN WITH YOU HANDS OR
GENITALS.
(What is this, a home castration kit?)

On a child's superman costume: WEARING OF THIS GARMENT DOES NOT ENABLE
YOU TO FLY.
(That's right, destroy a universal childhood fantasy!)

Illogical product
labels and
instructions.

VIRTUAL GOODS MAY EXIST ONLY IN VIRTUAL SPACE[3]

Cyberauctions such as those hosted by e-Bay allow consumers to sell and buy virtually anything they want—from collectibles, to cars, to eggs harvested from supermodels (shown in the illustration on p. 110). The popularity of cyberauctions
attests to their usefulness to consumers. However, there is little monitoring to

No money-back guarantee.

ensure standards of quality and authenticity of the items offered for sale. Consumers must be aware that fraud, counterfeit goods, and stretching of truths accompany cyberauctions. Unfortunately, not all virtual goods purchased at cyberauctions will materialize into actual goods.

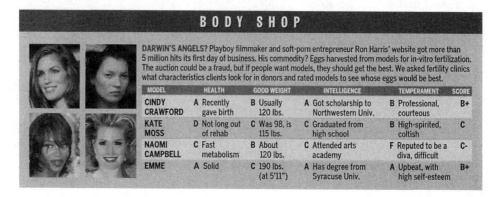

BODY SHOP

DARWIN'S ANGELS? Playboy filmmaker and soft-porn entrepreneur Ron Harris' website got more than 5 million hits its first day of business. His commodity? Eggs harvested from models for in-vitro fertilization. The auction could be a fraud, but if people want models, they should get the best. We asked fertility clinics what characteristics clients look for in donors and rated models to see whose eggs would be best.

MODEL	HEALTH	GOOD WEIGHT	INTELLIGENCE	TEMPERAMENT	SCORE
CINDY CRAWFORD	A Recently gave birth	B Usually 120 lbs.	A Got scholarship to Northwestern Univ.	B Professional, courteous	B+
KATE MOSS	D Not long out of rehab	C Was 98, is 115 lbs.	C Graduated from high school	B High-spirited, coltish	C
NAOMI CAMPBELL	C Fast metabolism	B About 120 lbs.	C Attended arts academy	F Reputed to be a diva, difficult	C-
EMME	A Solid	C 190 lbs. (at 5'11")	A Has degree from Syracuse Univ.	A Upbeat, with high self-esteem	B+

COOKIES TRACK

When consumers visit web sites, little bits of text called "cookies" are often left on their hard drives. These cookies are identification tags that allow companies to track the consumer's Internet travels and collect information on them: what sites they visit, how long they stayed, and what they looked at. By tracking consumers, companies get to know them better and thus are in a position to serve them better. It seems like a win-win situation. However, consumers often do not know they are being tracked or that volumes of information are being collected on them, some of which may be erroneous and potentially harmful. Cookies are consumer footprints without a face. As soon as consumers fill out Internet forms or web companies combine forces with direct marketing firms, however, the owners of the footprints are identified: name, address, phone number, and more.[4]

Your cookie crumbs leave a trail.

In the fairy tale, Hansel and Gretel left a trail of bread crumbs on purpose so they could find their way back home after their travels in the forest. When consumers visit web sites, they may have no idea that they are leaving a trail of cookie crumbs and are being tracked.

REFERENCES

Chapter 1: Introduction

1. Tom, Gail, & Ruiz, Susan. Everyday low price and traditional price, *Journal of Psychology*, July 1997, Vol. 131, No. 4, pp. 401–406.
2. McMath, Robert M., *What were they thinking?* New York: Times Business, 1998.
3. Williams, Geoff. Suckers! *Entrepreneur*, August 1999, pp. 95–105.
4. Lardner, James. Your every command, *U.S. News & World Report*, July 5, 1999, pp. 44–46.
5. Peppers, Don, & Rogers, Martha. Lessons from the front, *Marketing Tools*, Jan/Feb. 1998, pp. 39–42.

Chapter 2: Perception

1. Don't use this lemon for lemonade, *Sacramento Bee*, July 15, 1982.
2. Tom, Gail, Barnett, Teresa, Lew, William, & Selmants, Jodean. Cueing the consumer: The role of salient cues in consumer perception, *Journal of Consumer Marketing*, Spring 1987, Vol. 4, No. 2, pp. 23–27.
3. Cowley, Geoffrey, & Springen, Karen. Is there a sixth sense? *Newsweek*, Oct. 13, 1997, p. 67.
4. Bishop, Jerry E. Sixth-sense therapy path to be reported: Data hints humans can get chemical messages, *Wall Street Journal*, April 11, 1996.
5. Chandler, Susan. Under the gun at Dayton Hudson, *Business Week*, May 20, 1996, p. 70.
6. Tysoe, M. What's wrong with blue potatoes? *Psychology Today*, December 1985, pp. 6–8.
7. White, H. Name change to Rusty Jones helps polish product's identity, *Advertising Age*, February 18, 1980, pp. 47–50.
8. Tom, Gail, Dragics, Michelle, & Holdregger, Christi. Using visual presentation to assess store positioning: A case study of J.C. Penney, Marketing Research, September 1991, pp. 48–52.
9. *Dateline NBC*, 1996.
10. Underhill, Paco. *Why we buy*, New York: Simon & Schuster, 1999.
11. Tom, Gail, Burns, Michael, & Zeng, Yvette. Your life on hold: The effect of waiting time on consumer perception, *Journal of Direct Marketing*, Summer 1997, Vol. 11, pp. 25–31.
12. Tom, Gail, & Lucey, Scott. A field study investigating the effect of waiting time on consumer satisfaction, *Journal of Psychology*, November 1997, Vol. 131, No. 6, pp. 655–660.

Chapter 3: Motivation

1. Berger, David. Theory into practice: The FCB grid, *European Research*, Jan. 1986, pp. 35–46.
2. Vaughn, Richard, How advertising works: A planning model, *Journal of Advertising Research*, February-March 1986, pp. 57–66.
3. Edwards, Betty. *Drawing on the right side of the brain*, J. P. Tarcher, September 1999.
4. McDaniel, Carl, & Gates, Roger. *Contemporary marketing research*, 1st ed., 1991.
5. Alsop, Ronald. Advertisers put consumers on the couch, *The Wall Street Journal*, May 13, 1988.

Chapter 4: Learning and Memory

1. Reilly, Rick. The Swooshification of the world, *Sports Illustrated*, February 24, 1997, Vol. 86, No. 8, p. 78.
2. Duffy, Tara Suilen. Lacoste, crocodile battle for reptile trademark, *Sacramento Bee*, Oct. 14, 1999.

3. McMath, Robert M. Image counts, *American Demographics*. May 1998, p. 64.
4. McMath, Robert M. Selling the wrong image, *American Demographics*. August 1998, p. 80.
5. McMath, Robert M. *What were they thinking: Marketing lessons I've learned from over 80,000 new product innovations and idiocies*. New York: Random House, 1998.

Chapter 5: Attitude and Attitude Change
1. Beckwith, Harry, *Selling the invisible*, New York, Warner, 1997.
2. Tom, Gail, & Eves, Anmarie. The use of rhetorical devices in advertising, *Journal of Advertising Research*, July/August 1999, Vol. 39, No. 4, pp. 1–5.
3. Catanescu, Codruta, & Tom, Gail. Types of humor in television and magazine advertising, *Review of Business* (forthcoming).
4. Cialdini, R. B., Vincent, J. E., Lewis, S. K., Catalan, J., Wheeler, D., & Darby, B. L. Reciprocal concessions procedure for inducing compliance: The door-in-the-face technique, *Journal of Personality and Social Psychology*, 1975, No. 31, pp. 206–215.
5. Reigen, P. H. On inducing compliance with requests, *Journal of Consumer Research*, 1978, No. 5, pp. 96–102.
6. Burger, J. M., Increasing compliance by improving the deal: The that's-not-all technique, *Journal of Personality and Social Psychology*, 1986, No. 51, pp. 277–283.
7. Freedman, J., & Fraser, S. Compliance without pressure: The foot-in-the-door technique, *Journal of Personality and Social Psychology*, 1966, No. 4, pp. 195–202.
8. Cialdini, R. B., Cacioppo, J. T., Bassett, R., & Miller, J. A. Low-ball procedure for producing compliance: Commitment then cost, *Journal of Personality and Social Psychology*, 1978, No. 36, pp. 463–476.

Chapter 6: Personality and Self-concept
1. Etcoff, Nancy. *Survival of the prettiest: The science of beauty*, New York: Doubleday, 1999.
2. Quick, Harriet. *Catwalking*, Edison, NJ: Book Sales, 1999.
3. Gross, Michael. *Model*, New York: Warner, 1996.
4. Mulvey, Kate, & Richards, Melissa. *Decades of beauty*, New York: Checkmark Books, 1998.
5. Farrell, Greg. How IBM has managed to build a completely new corporate image, Gannett News Service, *Sacramento Bee*, November 8, 1999.

Chapter 7: Small Groups and Word-of-Mouth Communication
1. Walker, Chip. Word of mouth, *American Demographics*, July 1999, pp. 30–40.
2. Smith, Geoffrey. Sneakers that jump into the past, *Business Week*, March 13, 1999, p. 71.
3. Reitman, Valerie, This muscle car fairly screams out: You wanna drag? *Sacramento Bee*, Jan. 25, 1998.
4. Gladwell, Malcolm. *The tipping point*, Boston: Little, Brown and Company, 2000.
5. Park, Alice. A weird case, baby? Uh huh! *Time*, June 28, 1998, p. 41.

Chapter 8: Subcultures
1. Stanley, Thomas, & Danko, William, *The millionaire next door*, New York: Simon & Schuster, 1998.
2. Dacyczyn, Amy. *Tightwad gazette: Promoting thrift as a viable alternative lifestyle*, New York: Random House, 1993.
3. Dacyczyn, Amy. *The complete tightwad gazette: Promoting thrift as a viable alternative lifestyle*, New York: Random House, 1999.
4. McDonald, Marci. Down and out in Silicon Valley, *U.S. News & World Report*, July 19, 1999, pp. 28–40.
5. Conlin, Michelle. Valley of no dolls, *Business Week*, March 6, 2000, pp. 126, 129.
6. Tom, Gail, Garibaldi, Barbara, Zeng, Yvette, & Pilcher, Julie. Consumer demand for counterfeit goods, *Psychology & Marketing*, August 1998, Vol. 15, No. 5.
7. McGinn, Daniel & Halpert, Julie Edelson. Driving Miss Daisy—And selling her the car, *Newsweek*, Feb. 3, 1997, p. 14.
8. Dent, Harry S. Jr. *The great boom ahead*, New York: Hyperion, 1993.
9. Coupland, Douglas. *Generation X*, New York: St. Martin's Press, 1996.
10. Goff, Lisa. Don't miss the bus! *American Demographics*, August 1999, pp. 49–54
11. Wellner, Alison. Gen X homes in, *American Demographics*, August 1999, pp. 57–62.
12. http://www.troutman.org/humor/genx.htm/; http://www.dodds.net/~zeke/funnyfiles/misc/Gen X-Lingo.txt; http://irenaeus.ccsu.ctstateu.edu/~www/humor/miscellaneous/gen-x-glossary.html
13. Chaplin, Heather. Food fight! *American Demographics*, June 1999, pp. 64–65.
14. Faust, Kimberly, Gann, Michael, & McKibben, Jerome. The boomlet goes to college, *American Demographics*, June 1999, pp. 44–45.

Chapter 9: Culture

1. Ekman, Paul, & Friesen, Wallace. *Unmaking the face*, Englewood Cliffs, NJ: Prentice-Hall, 1975.

2. Lowe, Jaime. Comic-kraze, *Maxim*, March 2000, p. 54.

3. Hatfield, Elaine, Cacioppo, John T., & Rapson, Richard L. *Emotional contagion*, Cambridge, MA: Cambridge University Press, 1994.

4. Axtell, Roger E. *Do's and Taboos Around the World*, New York: Wiley, 1984.

5. Schwartz, Joe. Hispanic opportunities, *American Demographics*, May 1987, pp. 56–59.

6. Baleja, Gregory. http://rowlf.cc.wwu.edu:8080/~n9243762/humor/translations.

7. Murphy, Kate, Gifts without gaffes for global clients, *Business Week*, Dec. 6, 1999, p. 153.

8. Levine, Robert, V. The pace of life, *American Scientist*, September-October, 1990, Vol. 78, pp. 450–459.

9. Levine, Robert, V. The pace of life in 31 countries, *American Demographics*, November 1997, pp. 20, 23, 25, 27, 29.

10. Springen, Karen. Measuring up: It's not a small world after all, *Newsweek*, May 11, 1998. p. 12.

11. Ono, Yumiko. Pizza in Japan is adapted to local tastes, *Wall Street Journal*, June 4, 1993, p. B1.

12. Reitman, Valerie. India anticipates the arrival of the beefless Big Mac, *Wall Street Journal*, October 25, 1993, pp. B1, B5.

13. Penteado, J. R. Whitaker. Fast food franchises fight for Brazilian aficionados, *Brandweek*, June 7, 1993, pp. 20–24.

14. http://www.auburn.edu/~solommr.

Chapter 10: The Consumer Decision Process

1. Tverksy, A., & Kahneman, D. The framing of decisions and the psychology of choice, *Science*, 1981, No. 211, 453–458.

2. Kahneman, D., & Tversky, A. Choice, values and frames, *American Psychologist*, 1981, pp. 341–350.

3. Levin, I. P., Johnson, R. D., Russo, C. P. & Deldin, P. J. Framing effects in judgment tasks with varying amounts of information, *Organizational Behavior and Human Decision Processes*, 1985, pp. 362–377.

4. Underhill, Paco, *Why we buy*, New York: Simon & Schuster, 1999.

Chapter 11: "How to Fool Consumers" or "Caveat Emptor"?

1. Collected over various sites and publications.

2. http://curmudgeon.freeservers.com/labels.html

3. Body shop, *Time*, November 8, 1999, p. 31.

4. Green, Heather, Alster, Norm, Borrus, Amy, Yang, Catherine. Privacy: Outrage on the Web, *Business Week*, Feb. 14, 2000, pp. 38–40.

INDEX

CREDITS AND ACKNOWLEDGMENTS

Chapter 1
4: © 1995 Mattel, Inc. All Rights Reserved.

Chapter 2
9: (all) Courtesy of Gail Tom. **10:** (top left and top right) Courtesy of Gail Tom.
10: (bottom) Created by cartoonist W. E. Hill, originally published in *PUCK* in 1915 as "My Wife and My Mother-in-law."
11: (all) Created by cartoonist W. E. Hill, originally published in *PUCK* in 1915 as "My Wife and My Mother-in-law."
12: Created by cartoonist W. E. Hill, originally published in *PUCK* in 1915 as "My Wife and My Mother-in-law."

Chapter 3
31: Two illustrations adapted from N.A. Weisstein & E. Wong, 1986. Figure ground organization and the spatial and temporal responses of the visual system. In E.C. Schwab & H.C. Nusbaum (Eds.), *Pattern recognition by humans and machines.* Volume 2. Visual perception (pp. 31–64). Orlando: Academic Press. **32:** Reprinted with permission of Dow Jones & Co., from "The Mind of a Roach Killer," *The Wall Street Journal*, May 13th, ©1988, p. 19. Permission conveyed through Copyright Clearance Center, Inc.

Chapter 4
40: AP Photo/Anat Givon.

Chapter 6
65: (top) Perception Laboratory, University of St. Andrews.

Chapter 9
92: 4 Facial Expressions, ©1975 Paul Ekman/Human Interaction Laboratory, University of California, San Francisco.
97–98: Robert L. Levine, "The Pace of Life," *American Scientist,* September–October 1990, vol. 78, pp. 450–459. Reprinted with permission. **99:** Computer Generated Ethnic Blends: Photos by Ted Thai for Time, computer morphing by Kin Wah Lam, design by Walter Bernard & Milton Glaser. ©Time, Inc. All rights reserved.
103: www.auburn.edu/~solommr/ From Michael R. Solomon, Auburn University, AL 36849.

Chapter 10
110: "Body Shop," November 8, 1999, p. 31. ©1999 Time, Inc. All rights reserved.
110: (top left) Honda/AFP. **110:** (top right) Richard Drew/AP Photo. **110:** (bottom left) Luca Bruno/AP Photo. **110:** (bottom right) Michael Paras/AP Photo.